Love Unvoiced

An Anthology Curated by

Lokeshna Bulani

Inkfeathers Publishing
www.inkfeathers.com

Love Unvoiced
Edited & Compiled by Lokeshna Bulani
Print Edition

First Published in India in 2022
Inkfeathers Publishing
New Delhi 110095

All rights reserved.

ISBN 9789390882472

www.inkfeathers.com

Featuring the writings of

Gauri Agarwal, Shubhang Sharma, Sanaskriti Saha, C. Dave

Asmi Deshpande, Anvi Gupta, Vedika, Tiara Mehrotra

Aksheeta Chandok, Laveena Chandnani, Harshvi Soni

Tanisha Joshi, Sumedha Pant, Muskan Sahani, Garv Archana

Bhoomika Aggarwal, Srishti Sareen, Rakhee Daryanani

Vaneeta Chugh, Tanushree Dewanjee, Madhuchhanda Das

Ria Gandhi, Varsha Mahipal, Namoe, Nikunj Goyal, Dev Sahu

Bedavalli Misra, Priya Debnath, Didriksha Chakraborty

Apoorva Ravi, Mansi Kothekar, Vaishnavi Zinjad

Veena Antony, Szuati Dube, Anu Thampy, Nilesh Mandhyan

Sandhita Agarwal, Harshita Gupta, Vansh Aggarwal

Mansi Valera, Samarpuneet Kaur Sandhu

Bhumika Khandelwal, Chirkankshit Bihari Bulani

Disclaimer

The anthology 'Love Unvoiced' is a collection of 10 stories, 7 articles and 46 poems written by 43 authors who belong to different parts of the world.

Unless otherwise indicated, all the names, characters, objects, businesses, places, events, incidents- whether physical/non-physical, real/unreal, tangible/ intangible in whatsoever description used in this book are either the product of the author's imagination or used in a fictitious manner. Any resemblance to actual persons, objects, entities, living or dead, or actual events is purely coincidental.

The stories, articles and poems published in this book are solely owned by their respective authors and are in no way intended to hurt anyone's religious, political, spiritual, brand, personal or fanatic beliefs and/or faith, whatsoever. In case, any sort of plagiarism is detected in the stories, articles and poems within this anthology or in case of any complaints or grievances or objections, neither the anthology editor nor the publisher is to be held responsible.

I want to dedicate this book to
Lord Shiva and Goddess Parvati
for having the first love marriage in the universe
and to Radha and Lord Krishna for bringing the first story of
complete yet incomplete love to the world,
giving birth to the idea of love,
both with and without marriage.

Contents

Meet the Editor

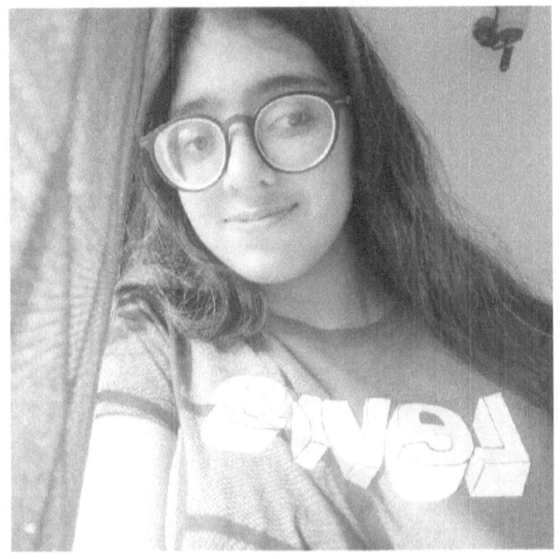

Lokeshna Bulani

Always up for deep conversations, Lokeshna is a sixteen-year-old student from the city of love, Agra. She is an aspiring poet and writer. She has been writing for her school magazine since she was nine, and thus was born her passion for writing. She is a published author, and this is her first anthology. A daydreamer, she believes in old-school love and finds her peace in herself. She thinks that everyone should skip achievements in introductions and start looking for ideas. Her introspective nature lets her discover new things about herself every single day. You can connect with her on Instagram at @bibliophilemaniac_.

Preface

This book is an amalgamation of many ideas, imaginations, and true stories. It strings words into small, beautiful pieces which will leave the reader longing for more. I wanted to curate this book to bring together the wordings of numerous lovelorn souls, each explaining what love is in their own unique ways. Everyone writes about love — love they met, love they lost or the love they felt. But these aren't just love stories. They are way more tragic and dramatic than that. Love is something everyone knows something about and has interpretations about. Love is somewhat indescribable on the whole. This book aims to describe the indescribable to some extent. Every co-author has found versatile ways to express themselves making this theme their own.

The new people I met throughout the making of this book made me look at love in very different, new ways and brought in fresh and innovative ideas to add to the book. Every write-up I went through during the editing process had its own aroma, a tale to tell. I learnt that I won't always be correct or wrong. Life is a balance of the right and wrong, and karma makes you compensate for all your deeds.

It feels like a dream to hold this book in my hand with my name shining on the cover. It takes me back to the days in grade four when I used to write numerous short stories and later make them one, connecting one character to the other. My writing journey began with an autobiography of a couch in a doctor's house. Since then, I started writing articles, stories, thoughts, and many other things for my school magazine, and it honed my writing skills a lot, which later helped me get published and is also one of the major reasons this book exists. Anthologies have always been my preference over long novels as it brings new ideas every few minutes during reading.

With this book, I grew into a more mature person, and I was able to find the right fit for me. I developed into a better human being, embracing new values in myself. Love doesn't always remain unvoiced; sometimes, it brings to you a new, happier version of yourself. I became that version of myself this year with all the love and constant support I got. It's been a rollercoaster in the creation of this book, but I never lost hope; maybe, that is what counts and it made me reach where I am today. In the making, my favourite part was to go through the entries and know the writer's intent behind those words. Readers can expect to find a variety of love — thoughts throughout the book, each leading to an unforgettable ending. To sum up, it was a great experience.

Hope you enjoy reading this book as much as I enjoyed bringing it to life.

Love,
Lokeshna Bulani

Let Your Insanity Sink In

by Srishti Sareen

Will you ever know what love is? Will you ever find the actual, raw, and true definition of love in this world? No one can, but it has something deeper within it. Behind a movie with imperfect flaws, a poet's last word in her poem, a lyricist's first note synced on the guitar string, a huge, monumental gesture, the toe of a dancer caressing the stage, or maybe an artist's asymmetrical crease on the canvas could be love. Is it something you want or something you learned already the moment you took your first breath? Only you know what love makes you feel in real life.

Love can make you do stupid, reckless things that you will regret at some point in your life. Still, you will do it anyway because that's what love is. What about the young love that has no destination? The electric rush will make your tummy tickle and cheeks turn red. The minute you both catch the first sight; it could be the reason for something that will last longer than a day-old coffee. Will it ever be classic, old, like a fine wine stored somewhere far away in a wooden barrel? Maybe the only possibility of having love in your life is just like an almost cold pizza, winter's first breeze, autumn's last golden leaf, or a fading rose next to an unknown grave. From the ink dried on the old pale paper under the lantern till the time text is typed on an android somewhere in this world, there is love that never dies. The world changed, science and technology reached heights. The meaning of love prospered too. Pure romantic tales took birth and died decades ago, but there is always a room where the romance began for the first time. Walls that belonged to them, a room on the extreme right corner where the wooden floors creaked, somewhere down the alley a house where an almost broken porch is still there. The one where a young girl shared her first kiss or the couch while his fingers softly slid under her skirt and made her clench the cushions which tried to cover her legs that were far apart. Love is nothing but a reminder of something that can never be relived but is always cherished. Some expired dates and days that never lasted past 1:04, forgotten days they had candle night dinners on are also a part of love. Yet, love is scandalous, breath-taking, and somehow alive, but it can go down the hill anytime. It can disappear in the blink of an eye. Love could never be left aside but still, be fragmented at its own pace. It will always be on the brink of vulnerability. It is one of the most tragic yet fulfilling feelings in the world.

Love is passionate but never consistent. Someone could feel the gap in romantic relationships and just like that the almost perfect love story will lose its purpose and at that very instant, there would be nothing left to cling to. It will just be an end that no one is destined to conquer. The tales of love are filled with layers of triggers – the ones that can soon be peeled and be out in the open, naked with its last breath. But there will always be stillness and calm when one is in love. No matter how painful or chaotic love can be; one will always crave for more. One would always have someone who will be there maybe or their not so lost forever because there will always be a side of the coin that will never be flipped. Humans can never let go of the feeling of love.

Love is the bread and butter to a hungry soul so one can never be full of it. You can never forget the first touch, the touch of that person who makes you curl up your toes, the one who is your home. It is the touch that can neither be carved on your body nor can be forgotten. All it provides you is warmth, comfort, long hugs, and soft kisses. It feels like a warm breakfast cooked for a chilly Sunday. It will always be more than the anatomy of the human body. Love is something that lets you sink into the underbelly of something unknown. It's something that is beyond the scars, fright, lust, and greed, the kind of love that lets you snuggle up like a ball of fur. The bottle of ink could dry, one can run out of the sheets of paper, but one can never be out of the words for the language of love, love that is celebrated, the one that saw the destruction and wars, melting ice, and burning forests. The love that will somehow find a way to outshine itself in its own dirty little twisted way through almost broken hourglass and a hundred uneven shades of the sky. Love is mixed up with purity and innocence, madness, and stillness. It somehow could be unrequited but there will be times when love is unforgettable. Love is a tale that will drive you insane and you will wilfully let your insanity sink in.

Always Been A Conundrum

by Anu Thampy (KrystlChaos)

Is love irrational?

Or

Is it that unconventional spice which adds

meaning to our existence?

Is it the rock we place our belief in?

Or

Is it just a silver lining we look forward to?

Is it that clutter you feel when there are no words

to gauge your emotions?

Or

Is it the comfort you feel when you have a whole room to vent

every bit of despair you are going through?

Does it reside in that silent whisper of strength

when you were terrified?

Or

A home you felt within that shoulder you cried back on?

Is it everything that you want in life?

Or

Is it the missing piece you need badly to feel complete?

Is love in those tears rolling down when you

confront the question of losing it?

Or

Is it in that laughter you slipped out within

every millisecond in the presence of it?

Does it matter if love exists?

Or

Is it everything you would bet on?

Is it worthwhile to give away a lifespan towards seeking it?
Or
Is our life shorter to experience the whole of it?

Can you see it wherever your eyes reach out to?
Or
Just in that place where you were looking for?

Does it mean there is nothing greater than love?
Or
Does every other emotion reside in it?
Within those depths of love.

If I Tell You

by Anu Thampy (KrystlChaos)

If I tell you I was wrong;
would you treat me like a sinner?

If I tell you, you were right;
would you know how it hurt me?

If I tell you, I wish I were dead;
would you whisper a quote of strength?

If I tell you, I knew the truth;
would you be disloyal to me as well?

If I tell you, I fell into the pit;
would you turn back and leave?

If I tell you, I cried and never stopped;
would you let me feel your heartbeat?

If I tell you, I couldn't be stronger;
would it mean my soul is too fragile?

If I tell you, I hate you;
wouldn't you doubt it for a second?

If I tell you, I love you;
would you look me in the eye and let me believe it?

Only if I tell you...

Rest In Peace, Love
by Asmi Deshpande

My love for you has died.

Darling,

You gave me what you had

I tried to give you the same,

But now

You'll see my love buried in Earth.

I wrote it for you

But it has already ended up in flames.

I killed my feelings for you

There's blood everywhere,

And tears of regret

My love for you was a letter that never reached your heart

My love for you was like a sandcastle that was ruined by the
ocean.

An Untold Fondness

by Madhuchhanda Das (Madhu)

The untold words bring back to me fond memories of my childhood school days, memories I hold so dearly and unforgettable love to cherish forever, a journey worth remembering. I and my best buddy never realised this for ages. We parted our ways in the humdrum of life and never bothered to nurture our friendship. During our school days, we didn't speak much but when I would need help for submitting my projects, my homework and sometimes class notes, I always knew 'he' was the person who would come up and lend a helping hand no matter what.

Back during the 1990s when we were in school, I still remember his voice when he used to stand up and answer all the questions asked by the teacher and look into my eyes even while answering. I can never forget how sad I used to feel when he didn't turn up on some days. Naughty and nice we were both to each other that strengthened our bond.

So many years of not being together finally revealed 'In a heartbeat, I will keep choosing you, without a doubt, without a pause'.

I know about his silent care, even though he never expressed his feelings, and it would remain like this forever.

The teachers separated us and made us sit on a different bench, but he always used to come back as soon as the class got over. It seems so stupid nowadays, but it was never stupid at that point of life, the beautiful past that created golden memories to be cherished forever.

That is the reason which makes us think that school friends are so stupid yet so special. These are lifetime memories that will surely treasure when old age comes. Reconnecting with him is like a medicine for a wounded heart and vitamin for a hopeful soul. I wish this goes on unexpressed forever, because it is where the beauty of this love lies.

Daffodils

by Harshita Gupta

Clear blue skies,
Silly smiles,
Cotton clouds floating above our heads,
Like a kid daydreaming but at night.
No signs of rain,
For a cuckoo sings with all its might.
And you ask me,
"Have you ever been in love?"
The world around me disappears
In the blink of an eye.
The mushy smell of ink and paper surrounds me,
For I've loved someone so desperately
That it reminds me of a poet
Searching for the first words of his poetry.

Waiting for a glimpse of his,
I watch the purple lilacs slowly yet steadily
Smell like him.
The tinkling sound of the bicycle bell
Feels like it has replaced the air,
Surrounding me.
There you arrive,
With a silly smile pasted on your face.
A smile so beautiful,
That it would compel an artist
To paint you with the shades,
Pink, purple and red.
Representing love,
For the air surrounding me,
Diffuses it perfectly!
You say "Hi" and your words feel like
I've been riding white horses in the clouds,
Following my heart, chasing my dreams,
Running in a race,
Only to reach you at the end of my day.

Staring at the yellow acacia,
I've been hiding all this while,
You smile and I lose my sight.
"For your secret love," you say
And I blush as if the roses were raining
From the sky.
I wake up from my daydreams.
This world surrounds me, again.
With you staring at me,
Waiting for my answer,
The answers you never gave me.
"Daffodils," I say
"This represents the love, the love that made him my poetry."

Summers In My City

by Harshita Gupta

The last day, the last call
The early sun enters the view
With its rosy hues.
Moon departs with its grief-case
Bidding us adieu.
Blue, it's all blue.
I wait for you at the bus stand
One last time
To find my peace in your grainy golden eyes.
Blue skies, dotted with fluffy white clouds
Drifting lazily.
I see you walking towards me
Like the summers in my city.

While jaded souls wander around the streets,
Waiting to be wrapped in the arms of shady trees,
I wait to be drenched
In the shadows of your smile.
For it's my soul that loves you,
This heart never accepted the truth.
You exist in moments,
You belong to my memories.
Bleeding sun recites the love stories
Of you and me.
Evening sun comes down on its knees,
While I hold my breath
And count to three.
You feel my gaze and my racing beats
While your soul asks,
What's wrong with me?
This soul hesitates but this heart,
It knows no boundaries.
Here's a confession: It speaks regardless
Whatever souls are made of,
Ours was never the same.
Just like poetry,
Everyone reads it with different names.

But this poetry,

Starts with the first letter of your name.

Moon arrives again,

Switching its grief-case with me.

Welcome to the mess in my head,

It has everything except peace.

Silence of the stars surrounds me,

While I wake up from another foolish dream.

Where my soul wants you,

This heart confesses what's true,

But all this time,

L-ove was the demon in our story,

Which is spelled as ove-L,

A story always meant to be doomed,

A tragic story of you and me.

Lovers Through The Screens
by Harshita Gupta

I search for you through the screens,
This house no more feels like home
Everything's a bit new to me.
This screen knows no trees, autumn leaves and blooming
flowers,
They wither searching for a new life
For this one feels like an incomplete tragedy.
Darkness swallows me,
While I struggle with the new normal
Searching for a home
Migrating to different sites.
It reflects my misery,
Whenever the screen sighs!
Adjusting my glasses for the nth time
My eyes declare, they miss your sight.

Golden mornings turn down,

Evening pours its silent dew,

My soul dances with the shining stars

For I've finally found my moon in you.

You appear in front of me,

Tinted eyes, smiling as if you, too, missed me.

As if your heart called for mine,

From miles away, through the screens.

You ask,

"How does it feel to be alone yet not feel lonely?"

All I say,

"Just like that last leaf, full of hope,

still hanging on an autumn tree,

For it needs your touch to bloom,

In a world full of grief, pain, longing, and screens,

In our world of you and me!"

A Beautiful Tragedy

by Anvi Gupta

It was my first day of the new term in Vintrigal High. I was excited.

New term. New school. Everything was new!

Finally, I got a chance, a reason, to stop thinking about my messed-up past. Ah, I'd rather not talk about it. After all, no one likes to listen about the 'real major teen problems'.

So, getting back to my new high school. It was beautiful, big and sort of historic. People were kind, some were sportive, some were studious, and some were the combination of both, while some were rather strange, just like me.

The teachers, well, were teachers. I'd rather not say anything about them.

****

On my seventh day or so, I was sitting in the canteen, alone. I was stuffing my mouth as fast as I could. The bell for the next period was about to ring. I didn't want to be embarrassed in front of my teacher. Also, Isobel, my crush, was going to be in the same room.

I was running at bolt speed in the corridor. The history teacher was about to shut the door, but I was lucky enough to reach it in time.

Everyone was staring at me as I kept panting like a dog. Yeah, Isobel was staring at me, too. However, she was smiling. Even her single glance did wonders to me.

The teacher gave me a typical stare and asked me to sit next to Isobel. I turned red like a tomato. I took a seat and tried not to look at her. My whole body was going through euphoria. After all, who wouldn't be elated sitting next to their crush? The class soon got over. Those forty-five minutes felt like they got over in a fraction of seconds. I wanted that period to go on forever.

Everyone started leaving the class, so did I. Many of the boys and girls were approaching her. However, Isobel's eyes were looking at me. From right to left, left to right, she scanned the whole room. And there, she found me in the corner of the room, reading a book.

'Hey, Sylvie! I am Isobel.'

'Hey, Isobel.'

'How are you doing?'

'Well, I am doing really great after meeting you! How about y-'

'Me, too. I see you are new here in Vintrigal High. Do you mind meeting my friends?'

'Sure. But, how about we do that in the evening? I have to go to the next class. I am free later.'

'Oh, cool beans!' She tried not to look into my eyes.

'Meet you later.' I left.

****

I have this habit of biting my lips when I get anxious or nervous.

I bit my lip so sharply that it started bleeding. Anyway, I took my stuff for the next period and slid into the classroom. It was my art period. People said I was good at making portraits. Moreover, it used to be my favourite subject in the lower grades.

I was thinking about her. She was the most beautiful person I had ever met. Her soul was pure. Her milk-white skin was as soft as a teddy bear. The combination of her blonde hair, blue eyes, heart-shaped face, a seductive voice, and a petite, curvy body was heavenly. Anyone would fall for such an irresistible beauty. Adding to that, she was thoughtful to everyone. She was mature. She was an ace at studies and sports, both. To be precise, she was perfect.

And I, on the other hand, was just good at almost everything but art. My mom used to say I had magic in my hands. My masterpieces were so engaging, winsome, and prepossessing. No one could ignore my creations. Once my dad put them on the street. Then, I swear on God's name; the crowd there increased as if someone were giving away diamonds for free. I started drawing when I was eight. Now, I am seventeen and still making many chefs-d'oeuvre. *

The bell rang, and without heeding much, I collected my stuff. I was heading towards my locker, when suddenly Isobel crashed into me. All of my papers fell to the ground. She was helping me pick them up and saw a page. It said, 'I miss you, Mom and Dad.'

She abruptly looked up and discovered it was me. She was the first person to ignore any of my art pieces and, instead, heed any of my calligraphy.

She stared at it and asked, 'Where are your mom and dad?'

I did not reply to her and bowed my head down. My silence had already answered her question. I hurriedly left from there and went to my locker. After being done for the day, I exited the school through the fourth gate. I was returning back home.

Everything I looked at reminded me of my parents. Suddenly, someone came running from behind, and a strange hand fell on my back. I looked back and found it was her. I felt better.

She told me, 'Hey, I am so sorry for that incident.'

I smiled, 'It is alright. It wasn't your fault.'

Silence took over. The wind was blowing at an unusual pace, just like my heart was beating. We were walking down the street when a guy catcalled us. She remained silent, and her innocent eyes showed me her fear.

I went to him right away, infuriated and asked, 'What is it with you? Huh? Bastard!'

That big guy raised his left eyebrow and triumphed, 'Are you not afraid, kids?'

I turned towards Isobel and slowly whispered, 'When I hold your hand, run as fast as you can!'

I slapped the guy right on his face, held her hand, and we ran off, only to stop near her house.

'It was fun.' She said, panting

'Yeah, it really was…' I giggled.

'You look beautiful when you smile, Sylvie.' She said,

'Really? You, too.' We both blushed intensively.

'You are turning red,' we both said in unison and burst out laughing.

'Yeah? It is so cold outside. Let's go home?' I said.

'I would definitely have, but I got to go home. My mom would be waiting.'

'Sure!'

'Give me your phone. I'll feed my phone number in.'

I handed over my iPhone. She added her number to my contact list. After handing back me my phone, she waved at me and bid me goodbye.

****

I went inside my house. I looked at those walls that reminded me of Mom and Dad. This gave me peace, a memory of them; it made me feel as if they were there with me.

They were precious, and I wish they had never gone on that trip to Utah.

I was tired, so I soon retired to bed and dozed off after having dinner.

****

I woke up early the next morning like I usually did. But something was different that day. Instead of waking up reminiscing, I woke up smiling, thinking about my present. I was feeling loved again. However, I was afraid of this happiness going away from me again. I didn't want it to happen. All I needed was love and some happy moments with my favourite person. I had started loving her. It felt as if she knew every bit of me. As the days passed, our friendship grew stronger. I didn't know if she was crushing on me, too. We used to go to the park and have ice cream every day. We, as friends, enjoyed ourselves a lot.

And damn, that day! She came to me and confessed, 'I don't know how I should say this. But I really think I am in love with every square inch of your body. And your personality. It fancies me. Knowledge is not a question. Your way of talking just tells it all. And damn, that bold voice. It feels as if it were made just for that bitchy British accent of yours. The best part? It is the way you draw. It just feels so real, as if it has come to life.'

I stuttered, 'I –'

'Stay quiet. I have always been afraid of rejection. I'll just walk away. But, let me complete.'

'Listen to me, Isa...' I yelped. She fell silent.

'…After my parents died in an accident, I had been alone ever since you stepped into my life. You make me feel complete. I don't know what my life would be like without you. I have never been in a relationship. I was never ready to be in. Whereas I now know I need you. And I don't even want to imagine a life without you.'

She stared at me.

I stared at her.

She leaned in for a kiss and it was the best experience of my life. I kissed her back as if there was no tomorrow. I kissed her deeper, pushing her towards the nearest wall. Her soft hands were in one of mine, above her head. And another one on her waist, going down gently. She was reaching out to her neck and to her chest slowly.

We both were enjoying the holiest kiss of our life until she pulled back.

She hesitated, 'Sylvie before we go any further, I want to tell you something.'

'What is it?'

'Actually, um-'

'Tell me, Isa. You know you can trust me.'

'I know I can trust you. But you might feel played, or cheated. But trust me; I have really started to love you, Syl.'

I fretted, 'What do you mean?'

'You do know my friend Archie, right?'

'The tall, blonde brat?'

'Mm, yeah.'

'So, what does he have to do with it?'

'He gave me a dare to be in a relationship with you the day your papers fell... I know this sou-'

'Stop, Isobel. You ended it before it began. Tell me one thing, you seriously didn't think whatever you did was wrong? If all this was just a game, if you didn't really love me, why didn't you tell me the truth earlier?'

'I am so sorry for whatever I have done, Syl. I didn't tell you because I knew you'd have been hurt. I was looking for the right time. Over and above that, I had fallen in love with you. I fall for you deeper and deeper every day.'

I went numb as she spoke. I wanted to be alone. She knew that, too. Therefore, she left my house.

The other day, I didn't go to school. Instead, I went to a church in the town. I would always go there when I was sad. It is an antiquated building, victim of vandalism. No one used to go there anymore. Some wild daisies were growing there. Even though they were wild they looked beautiful. Isobel somehow knew I would be there. She came in through the back door and saw me caressing the scratched wall that quoted, *'Pulchra Tragoedia'**. I knew she was there. I remained silent. But she kept her hand on my shoulder. I could feel she was also hurt by that incident. I had a vibe.

She gently said, 'A beautiful tragedy.'

It was no news to me that she was a linguist; too. After all, she was an all-rounder. I smirked, 'A linguist, huh?'

She whispered, 'Yea. You doubt?'

I didn't reply.

I burst out crying.

I saw her eyes getting moist. I was sure she wanted to apologise. We both cried, embracing each other. I kept my head on her bosom. I cried for almost three hours, hugging her. I was grieving. I hadn't cried since the day my parents died. I was just taking it all in. But I could take it no more.

She kissed me again. I kissed her back, assuring her I trusted her. By sunset, we both came out of the church holding each other's hands. She came to my house. We shared my room and cuddled and kissed all night. And so, a new love story began.

Annotations-

Chef-d'oeuvre – masterpiece

'Pulchra Tragoedia'- beautiful tragedy (Latin)

Eres Mi Media Naranja*

by Chirkankshit Bihari Bulani

Her makeup didn't conceal her,
It revealed her.
When she stood, her arms stretched,
The camera stared at her, fully drenched.
I wish to bathe myself in her aura,
Surround myself with her voice,
Her love has made me a madman,
A patient of love with no choice.

Her makeup didn't conceal her,
It revealed her.
I look at my love, with so much curiosity,
My heart forgets all animosity.
I get in touch with all the colours,
While green and red hide like muggers.
I say, what can you rob me of?
What do I have to lose?

I played the game of dice,
The Yudhishthira* inside me knowing he has to lose.
I have lost this game of love, and my heart is no longer mine.

Her magic is beyond understanding,
It leaves you wanting.
She knows how to show half her face,
And kill me entirely.
Her eyes speak lines,
While her lips lay.
My heart was just down the lane,
But she didn't have to go that way.
Oh God, how did such lazy, get agile so fast?
Got his heart beating, and set his sail up the mast?

I shall not suffer this disease, for I will find a cure.
But till then, O my beating heart, you must endure.
Suffer this tantalising adventure with good in there,
Repair yourself when you see her.
I shall remain around my love, and gaze upon her hair.
And
I shall make my hypothesis
That,
Her makeup doesn't conceal her,
It reveals her.

Annotations-

Eres Mi Media Naranja – You're my other half (Spanish)

Yudhishtira - He was a part of the Indian epic, Mahabharata and lost all his property, brothers and his wife, Draupadi to his paternal brother, Duryodhana by losing in game of dice.

Lovelorn

by Vedika

The moment our eyes met
A strange emotion took over me
It all felt foreign
For the first time, it felt like time had paused
Thoughts not leaving my mind
You were my way to utopia
You felt like a forever to me
Without knowing what stars had in store for us
Thinking about you, left me with uncountable sleepless nights
I thought it was a new beginning
But time proved me wrong
With the time passed by
I started losing myself
I asked myself if I was perfect for you
But my heart never gave me an answer
It always brought all my insecurities before me
I cried myself every day

Whenever I met you
My mind and heart in a war
Countless times I felt to pour my heart out
And confess my feelings to you
But my fears never wanted me to do so
It always hurt,
But I felt helpless
Years later,
I was filled with regret
I had lost all my chances
I had lost you forever
In the end, all my dreams were a mirage.

First Love

by Varsha Mahipal (RedBellPepper)

I met you for a short time,
But I wanted it to be forever instantly
We spoke about yours and mine,
And I wanted that to be ours immediately.
The path we walked on together,
Still asks about you
The words we said to each other,
Still remind me of you.
I didn't know a short conversation with someone could etch
them in our mind forever,
But I know now that it's true… because of you.

The True Nature Of Love

by Dev Sahu

All your life, you seek love like a shelter. This is unconsciousness. Love itself is shelter. Do not seek shelter in love. You are eager to express your love towards someone or to get someone's love. This is unconsciousness. If you enshroud your existence with the feeling of divine love, then you need not worry about finding love. If you have attained this form of yourself, then others will yearn to get a drop of the nectar of love from you. You will not have to extend a needy hand for help in front of anyone for the alms of love. Then, all the poverty in your heart will vanish and it will be filled with happiness. Lust will disappear in love. The emptiness of the mind will be filled with the joy of love. All the cravings will be satisfied. Then, you will be complete in yourself.

If the love you were looking for is not there, it cannot be obtained. What was not there, how can it be obtained? If you don't get love even after making endless efforts, then you will lose faith in love. Then, love will be replaced by lust. The heart which was thirsty for love will now be filled with lust. This is what happens with unsuccessful lovers. If a deal is not made with one, then someone else will make a good deal. Love never happened between the two. And if there was love, neither the feeling of vengeance would have entered the mind, nor would you go on the path of adultery.

There is so much adultery in the world because people are untouched by power and cannot feel the presence and need of true love. One who experiences the divinity of love, all his ego, all his anger, all negativity dissolves in the divine and blissful feeling of that love. And suddenly, goodness comes in the conduct of that person and happiness enters his life. But before love flourishes in a person's life, it is destroyed. Because conditions apply before love. This coincidence will happen very rarely in the world when there is a confluence of two worthy lovers. When love happens between two lovers, only love remains; both the lover and the beloved merge into it; they become one. And the distinction between the lover and the beloved disappears. Radha becomes Krishna. Krishna becomes Radha. They both become equivalent with love and melody.*

Love is not a merely personal feeling, rather it is more than the basic nature of life. This is a fundamental quality of life. Love is not just an emotional attachment that needs to be expressed; love is a deep feeling of the mind to be felt. When your experience of life deepens, then love also starts manifesting in your mind. One who has love in life can enjoy life. And one who is in bliss can understand and feel love. You can love someone or find love in someone. Or you can love yourself. To be loving in yourself means that your joy flows from within you. Your love is your own feeling; it is not imported from outside. This is the purest form of love. Being in love means having sweetness in your life. To be in love means to be joyful in life. He who is in love will be merciful and compassionate. His experience of life will be deep. He will have a feeling of love for all living beings. He will be closer to nature. To be in love in life means to be free. Love liberates you from any bondage. It protects you from many evils.

Lack of love in a person's life creates unnecessary evils in him like jealousy, anger, guilt, violence etc. Love purifies the mind and purifies the heart by washing away all filthy feelings. A person who lacks love in life will suffer from negativity. Negative emotions and negative tendencies will dominate his life. Love plays an important role in becoming a good person. It is love that a person searches for all his life. He expects love in his family, relationships or from friends or his spouse. And if he does not get it from there, he finds love within himself. And that is self-love, the best love. It doesn't have to be expressed through words but shown through actions.

Your longest relationship in life is with yourself.
Only when you manage this relationship well can you manage your relationships with others.
~ Vex King, Good Life Good Vibes

Annotations-

**Radha and Krishna* are collectively known within Hinduism as the combined forms of feminine as well as the masculine realities of God. Krishna and Radha are the primeval forms of God and his pleasure potency, respectively, in several Vaishnavite schools of thought.

It is believed that Krishna enchants the world, but Radha enchants even him. Therefore, she is the supreme goddess of all and together they are called as Radha-Krishna.

A Love Mystery

by Didriksha Chakraborty

Hey, my crush
I wonder why
Whenever I see you, I always blush?
As soon as my day starts
Your thoughts fill my heart
I can see your illusion everywhere
But about this, you are unaware
Is this the illusion of love?
Playing with my mind and heart
I feel everything about you is perfect
I don't know by which trait of yours
I was particularly impressed.
I smile and giggle whenever I feel your presence
I am inebriated by your irresistible essence
In my dream, I often see myself standing beside you
Holding your hands with the utmost excitement
Thanks to my wishful thinking.

But suddenly, everything disappears
Within a second of blinking
Your slight glimpse is enough to make my day
I wish I could tell you all this, by the way
Why am I so afraid to lose you?
When you are not even mine
In the dark days of life, you're my only sunshine
How you feel for me is still a mystery
I just want us to have a wonderful chemistry.

Thank You, Dost

by Garv Archana

For Cookie

Scribbled thoughts and pages,
All long for freedom.
From the inkpots of mine,
To your heart's kingdom.
My mind has become a maze,
Fighting wars with my heart.
Mind wishes to overpower,
Heart wins this part.

I said it out to you,
Loudly on New Year's Eve.
Still, something was left,
For which I peeve.

Fighting my own battles,
Is a daily chore.
But still, those thoughts of you I have,
How can I ignore?
Whether you know or not,
But you matter the most.
At least to me,
Forever, mere dost*
I know I'm the most boring human
On this planet I inhibit.
Knowing the fact, you still
Stood by my side, closely knit.
Can't thank you enough,
For being the reason for my smiles.
I only wish for our friendship,
Walks together for miles.

Can I ask you something?
With my lips tied.
Will you please, stay forever
Till the day I have died?

Annotations-
Mere dost – My friend (Hindi)

Forever Dreams

by Garv Archana

The heart calls out
For some confessions to display.
From the ones months back,
To the ones of yesterday and today.

I wish I could have done sooner,
What I always wanted to do.
From never leaving your side,
To spending the day with you.

Sipping on a cup of chai*,
Dipping our feet in the Ganga*.
From running together at the ghats*,
To doing some kaands* and panga*

Love Unvoiced

Protecting you from creepy eyes,
Shielding you like my treasure.
Talking with you all day,
Being my biggest pleasure.

Eating malaiyyo* in the morning,
To walking hand-in-hand.
Stirring up fondness,
Like a magic wand.

But all these are nothing,
Just mere thoughts.
Of mine and my heart,
Forever they are lost.

Some dreams unfulfilled,
Crazy yet soothing.
Whenever hitting my mind,
Leave me thinking,

I live in dreams,
Of them being true.
Then
I live in a reality
Where I love you.

Annotations-
**Chai*: Tea (Hindi)
**Ganga:* A holy river in India (Hindi)
**Ghats*: Riverbanks (Hindi)
**Kaands and panga*: Mischievous activities (Hindi)

Ahana

by Apoorva Ravi

What goes on in the head of a young girl who is copying a math equation from the board while sitting alone on the first bench? The PUC boards are near, but is she competent enough?

Maybe yes, maybe not…

Is she lonely?

Maybe yes, maybe not…

For how long do you think has she been sitting on the first bench? With no one but her books to talk to. She enters the class just before the bell rings and leaves for home when it rings again in the evening. The lull of the classroom banter is behind her, and the math equation is before her, but she is lost in her own thoughts of Harry Potter's magical world, waiting to go back to her book, which was her comfort, her home.

"Ahana! Can you please tell me what was in the last line; ma'am rubbed it before she left. Ahana… Ahana!" A voice came in.

"Huh! Oh yes, Amritha I…I am not sure. Sorry!" Ahana exclaimed.

"Oh! It's okay, but what were you doing then, sitting in front?" Amritha asked.

"I wasn't paying attention, actually," she replied.

Amritha gave her a confused look but before she could say anything, Ahana left and proceeded towards home.

"Hey! How are you?" a voice came again.

Ahana stopped with a thud.

It was him. After a whole year. Aditya.

How she missed having those conversations with him, about how he wrote the exam copying from the boy who sat behind him, all through high school. She remembered having taken his autograph before school ended. And here he was today, talking to her.

"Well, how are you?" he said.

Words couldn't find their way through her mouth except for the silly smile that was plastered on her face.

"Um, I am good! How come you are here?" she replied.

"Oh! I got transferred to this college from the ISE board, you know how it was, and they were like blood-sucking vampires." He giggled.

"Oh, I know!" Ahana replied excitedly.

"Yeah, okay, see you around," he said.

"Of course, Bye! "

"Bye!"

The walk back home was magical; Ahana had never seen the sun smile so beautifully at her before…

11 years later

Ahana looked outside the window; her cat woke her up, licking her eyes. It was 6:45 a.m. and the world was waking up. She switched on her Spotify. Vance Joy's Riptide started playing and she was taken back three weeks ago. All she could do was think about the boy who had sent that song. Memories of Saahil would come back to her now and again. Watching YouTube songs with him through Google Meets and those long conversations they used to have or the conversations at a cosy cafe in Bangalore, well, she had it all. But now, nothing.

She suddenly jumped when a song by Lumineers, another song which he had shared, was playing on her mobile. She got up, wiping her tears to the phrase, "I belong with you, you belong with me, you are my sweetheart."

What went wrong? Well, she knew it but just couldn't reconcile with it. The fact that she loved him a lot but had still feared saying yes to him when he asked certain things. Was it not enough? What they shared, for her to marry and live with him and his mother? Maybe yes. But she was not sure. She just did not know what she wanted anymore. She wanted to be with him but feared losing herself. He seemed a bit rigid sometimes and that scared her. Yes, he had not imposed anything on her. But, what if in the future, there were nothing common between the two of them?

Angela by Lumineers started playing next and Ahana just started dancing to it without a care for the world. She knew she was this free-spirited person, and maybe, maybe there was someone else made for her, not him. But still, there was something special between the two. The two years they were together was a tumultuous ride — with highs and lows and multiple breakups in between. But this time, she knew there was no reconciliation.

She started clearing her old books and her slam book back from school days fell on her lap. And there lay the autograph of her first crush — Aditya! She smiled. She had come a long way. From just smiling at her crush and never telling him about her feelings to having a two-year relationship with Saahil was a journey. She was no longer the naive girl that she had been back in school.

Ahana suddenly started singing and dancing to the music, picked up her cat, and gave him a swirl dance to the beats of *Tune Kaha by Prateek Kuhad*, her favourite singer.

She had experienced life. But somewhere within her lay that little girl, who loved life, who, despite telling her cousins that she was not ready for love, was still longing for that special someone with whom she could lock her eyes in the crowd and forget about everything else.

Truth And Lie

by Nikunj Goyal (Mr. Talkinspire)

Truth is bitter,
Because you're scared of it,
And lie feeds on fear,
When you provide it.

Isn't life already short,
To always be a feast of lies,
Isn't life already short,
To bear the bitter truth of life?

Isn't life already short,
To live with regrets,
Doesn't it hurt,
Enduring that entire burden on your head?

Isn't fear magnificent
For regrets to feed on?
It kills you and your confidence,
Like a slow, torturing death.

Its prey breaks fully,
Like a dry leaf falling off a tree.
It forgets its artistry,
All strings break away from reality.

So why choose a bitter recipe to make,
Let truth be your mate.
Let's let go those strings holding you back,
Let go of the feeling you hate.

?

by Nikunj Goyal (Mr. Talkinspire)

Life's a lie,

Death is a forlorn truth.

But it isn't sweet,

Like the lie we pursue.

Isn't it the truth that we fear?

Isn't it the happiness that we desire?

Isn't it the fun that we chase?

But consequences are what we don't want to face.

We hope for a long life,

We try finding peace in lies.

We try searching for the afterlife,

But it turns cold on that side.

We hope for love,
We all want to be with our true love.
But love, it's a beautiful dagger
Which can make you bleed,
But heals too, on your will.

There is no heaven
There is no hell,
The soul can only have peace
Beyond this death.

Earth can be hell
Or it can be paradise,
It's your choice,
How you want to live your life.

A Child

by Nikunj Goyal (Mr. Talkinspire)

A child is an alluring being,
Like water in personality.
He takes shape according to
The environment you take him in.

Like water ends the suffering,
Of people having thirst.
Just like that a child brings joy
In life, it is enduring.

They can be silent like still water,
Furious like a tsunami,
Joyful like splashing water,
And sound pleasant like running water.

They have a heart like a delicate pearl,
Mindset like a crystal-clear river,
With deep depths through which you can,
See everything till the end.

It depends upon the elders,
To either maintain that river,
Till their last breath.
Or ignore it,
Which makes it noxious with time.

It depends on the elders,
If they craft that pearl to alter,
Or ignore it,
To let it become bolder.

A child's nature arises from an ocean,
Covers the area as long as visible.
It is shaped by pressure,
Just like a vessel created by a potter.

Bit by bit, that pressure builds up into a sculpture,
Formed according to elders.
But if isn't carved properly,
Then that child one day breaks completely.

If more is applied, it becomes like a stone.
If less is applied, then it falls down soon.
In an urge to discover, it looks towards others,
And builds itself up in a way that is taught by life.

But because of that way of life,
Sometimes he may not get it right.
So, with age, he starts to turn into hard ice.
Who might have some wrong
interpretations about life.

When Two Souls Meet

by Apoorva Ravi

Poorvi

She was nervous, but she decided to call him. His profile seemed interesting. Jodi 365 was a reliable app indeed. It did match her with a compatible person and didn't end her up with some boy of her caste, like other apps... She was excited to talk to him.

"Ah! I am scared!" sighed Poorvi. She had decided to make the first move. But what would he think? Would he like her voice? What would they talk about? Thinking about all of these things in mind, she dialled his number.

"Hello!" She was welcomed by a voice with a baritone she liked instantly. "Ah, hey! Is this Saathvik? I am Poorvi. I found your profile on Jodi 365," she spoke nervously.

"Oh, hi, Poorvi. How are you?" was the reply from the other side.

After a few minutes, Poorvi had an innocent smile on her face that made her mother wonder about what had happened suddenly, that after a phone call, her daughter was so happy.

****

Saathvik

"Saathvik, where are you?" A voice called.

"Coming, mom!" Saathvik replied.

He was pleasantly amused. He had not known that these matrimonial platforms really worked; others had not. This particular one – the one he still did not know much about. He was taken aback when she had called him. And he could sense her nervousness from the phone. She was restless, too. She had said, "What else?" after five minutes of continuous talking. She was musically inclined. He smiled at the way she had tried to hide her ignorance about the classical guitar, when he told he was learning it.

"Saathvik! Where are you lost in your thoughts? Food is ready." Mom called again.

He had completely forgotten all about food; he was not so hungry either, yet he went to the kitchen to serve himself, smiling at what he knew awaited him.

****

Poorvi

Poorvi was amused to see how her life had changed drastically since the first phone call she had with Saathvik. Texting and calling him was so intriguing to her. She never knew life could be so beautiful despite the pandemic. She felt so close to him. She could open up about everything. Except for one thing. She had not shared her depression with him. She did not know how he would react or if he would understand what she had been through. After days of talking and trying to know each other, both of them decided to meet at Lalbagh. But before that, some girly-talk needed to be done. So, Poorvi called up Natasha, her first cousin and the closest one to her and told her to come over.

"Hey, Poorvi!" Her cousin Natasha had arrived. They had been close since childhood and had shared every small thing – from boys to periods to makeup.

"Hi! Natasha, I wanted to tell you something. I like someone. I don't know if it's love…" She started telling her story to Natasha when she interrupted in between, her face lit up with surprise.

"Oh wow, Poorvi! So exciting! Is it Saathvik? Have you decided to meet him? Tell me all about it. Go on. Don't hide anything…" Natasha said, within a breath. Her series of questions made Poorvi more nervous.

"Um, don't laugh. I met him on a matrimonial site…" Poorvi trailed off.

"Poorvi, its fine. Meeting a person on a matrimonial site is not a taboo or something to be laughed about. Just tell me about him. I want to know."

"Okay then, I feel that he is someone like a close friend. Whenever he calls, I feel so ridiculously happy. And lately, I have been posting more of my singing videos on YouTube just because he likes the way I sing. I don't know if I am crazy."

"Ah-ha! That is the reason behind singing those romantic songs. I was wondering, Poorvi, how my sister had become so brave that she started uploading songs on YouTube!" Natasha exclaimed. "So, tell me, when are you meeting him?"

"Tomorrow. I don't know what to do. I am very scared, Natasha. What if he doesn't like me?"

"Poorvi, don't stress. Just tell me one thing: what do you want? Do you think you are ready for a relationship now? As far as I know, you are often quite sceptical about relationships."

"I know. But talking to Saathvik makes me feel that a relationship with him will be effortless. He makes relationships seem like a partnership, where there is friendship, love, and excitement."

"That's it, Poorvi! You don't have to worry about anything else, now. Just be yourself. And the universe will ensure things will go well." Natasha's reassurance made Poorvi feel more confident about herself.

"Ha-ha, you are so filmy." Poorvi giggled, throwing a pillow at her.

****

The Next Day

Poorvi dressed up in a red kurti and topped it with oxidised jewellery with minimal makeup to look her best. After all, this was the first time they were meeting, and she wanted to leave a good and lasting impression on Saathvik. She looked at her mother, who wished her all the best for her first meeting and left on her Activa. As soon as she reached the place, she found out that it was allowing only fifty people inside the park and it was currently full, and maybe for the next few hours they would need to wait if they wanted to get inside. She tried calling Saathvik, but he didn't pick up.

Saathvik reached within five minutes and looking at Poorvi and the board outside the park, he suggested that they go to the Banashankari Park to spend some time together. Poorvi was getting more nervous every second, but Saathvik's reassurance made her feel calm. She replied in affirmative and together on his bike, they went to the Banashankari Park. As Poorvi sat behind him on his bike, she felt a chill running down her spine as she could feel his warmth so closely, making small talks in between so she could divert her mind from her own negative voice.

Saathvik

Driving to the park on his bike, Saathvik was lost. He had been thrown off guard while talking to her all this time.

Talking to her for a month had been like a roller coaster ride. He felt like she was someone very sensitive. She used to share a lot with him. But he also had a feeling she was holding back. That she was scared about something. And he just wanted to protect her and shelter her from all her worries.

And today, she had unknowingly inched closer towards him while they were on his bike, and he was nervous. He had never been close to anyone for a very long time. Well, she was nervous, too; he could sense that. Her voice and her sweaty palms while they were so close were evident enough.

"Hey, Saathvik! This way..." She instructed him and he followed. Soon, they reached the park and found an empty bench. He had brought jalebis, an Indian sweet dish from her favourite BDA Complex and she was delighted to see them.

As Poorvi looked at her jalebis, he told her, "Poorvi, chill! Don't be so nervous. Guess what? I am nervous too. But, since we have been speaking for a month, let's forget that we are meeting for the first time."

"Okay." Poorvi smiled. She realised it was going to be fine.

Her simplicity and the way her eyes sparkled when she spoke, captivated Saathvik. He felt that he was quite quickly taking a liking to Poorvi's innocence and endearing nature. Looking at them from afar would make any onlooker think that they were close friends. Little did they know that they were two people meeting for the first time, equally nervous about what the other might be thinking.

"Saathvik, I don't know whether I should be saying this now. But I had psychotic depression in my college, and I thought you should know," Poorvi blurted out after a few minutes of talking when she couldn't hold it any longer. "I wanted to tell you this right away because I don't want this relationship to begin with lies and hidden truths."

He was taken aback. Never had he seen a person be so candid. She had said something he was trying to reconcile with for a long time, it seemed. His loved one had psychosis, too, and he could understand how she was feeling. He realised that she was someone special. Someone who might understand him better than anyone.

Poorvi had fingers crossed. She did not know what he was thinking. But then she saw it. A reassuring smile on his face – a feeling that made her realise that all would be fine. And maybe, he would understand her and be there with her in her journey of life.

"It's okay," he said.

And thus started a new chapter in both of their lives, a chapter where love wasn't defined by words, but shown through actions. Truly, that's what love really meant.

Love?

by Bhoomika Aggarwal

Love for me is something that can't be explained,
An undefined feeling for a lifetime phase.

Love is like an outlandish maze,
Love is in which there's no limit,
Sometimes it might be a complicated feeling that can be hard to admit.

When 'me' and 'you' is replaced by 'us',
When you have the same person holding onto you every time.
No matter what,
You have a "God bless you!" with every hiccup.

Love for me is something, which maybe, I feel for you,
A feeling that's not physical yet strong,
A feeling where nothing feels wrong,
Love is a feeling that lasts forever,
It is the only magic that never wanes, however.

Maybe it's every time when I think of you
Or
I should rather say it's love because of which I think about you.

Something beautiful,
Sometimes unexpected.
But every time when it's about love,
It doesn't matter how many words I add
For me love will still be indescribable.
An unexplained feeling forever that'll always be undefined.

A Broken Heart It Is!

by Bhoomika Aggarwal

A broken heart it is not a spilled cup of tea,
That you need to gather quickly.
Take your time to heal,
Take time to pick up your pieces,
And rebuild yourself even more beautifully.

It's okay to be a mess sometimes.
Take time to understand yourself.
It's completely fine to feel low from time to time.

Don't be too hard on yourself
A broken heart it is not a few fallen pearls,
That you need to collect.
Take time to calm down,
And do the wrong things which feel right sometimes without
any regret.

With time, like a flower, you'll surely bloom again.
Take time to rebuild a new you that'll make 'em insane.

A broken heart it is,
A broken you.
A new chance to add into you what was always there,
A chance to take risks, exploring an unknown part of yourself.

Maybe upgrading a level,
Or just like renovating, for example.
It'll take time,
Because a broken heart is not anything lesser than a delicate doll.
Take chances, gather courage,
Return more beautifully with absolutely no regrets.

Thought Of You Today

by Vaishnavi Zinjad (Vaish)

If only you can see my eyes now
You will read all the unsaid words
If only you can see through them
You will understand that for me you are my world

I thought of you with love today,
But that is nothing new.
I thought about you yesterday,
And days before that, too.
I think of you in silence,
I often utter your name.
All I have is our memories
And a picture in a frame.

If only you could see the smile on my face
When I receive your email
You will know that you have
Captured heaven, and not hell.

Round and round, I go
Never stopping in a continuous flow.
I hang out with numbers each
And every day, and nothing
Ever gets into my way.

Your memory is a keepsake,
With which I'll never part.
God has you in His keeping,
I have you in my heart.

Him – A Missing Presence

by Aksheeta Chandok (Ash)

I've often wondered why so many individuals choose to go without saying goodbye.

Perhaps it is more difficult to end a one-on-one relationship because they no longer care or because they care too much.

In true love, there are no goodbyes.

But, as far as I'm aware, they don't say goodbye because they know we won't be able to let them go, so they don't offer us a choice.

They should, however, emphasise to us that we must have the necessary strength to survive without them.

The second time around, it didn't feel any better.

Our love may have always been stronger, but the emotions were intense and so was the grief.

Even if I was telling my heart to mend its wounded self, I couldn't actually perform the brief.

My mind was muddled and gloomy, and the agony was excruciating.

I understand that seasons change, but did you have to make any adjustments as well?

They claim, "People are never the same. They simply show their genuine colours."

However, you stood out from the crowd. We both had our moments, and I used to think you were the only one who could make my heart skip a beat. But now, I'm convinced that the man I adored never existed. He donned the masks that my ex wished he could wear.

Is it possible that love will bring you down?

Even after the breakup, I was still the "love of his life" in the eyes of the world, but it was all a distant memory for us.

My life has been a constant source of doom and sorrow since that time.

The world appears to be devoid of everything.

You lit a fire in the depths of my spirit. It was the fuel's red-burning ignition. But you abandoned me, abandoned me in the dark and alone.

Everything is painted black, which I realised far too late.

I gave you the authority to empower me, but instead, you used it to tear me down. And, you know, it's as if I've loved someone but they haven't returned my feelings. Even when I'm dancing in the rain, I don't feel joy, and I don't feel the same peace in my heart when I'm out at 3 a.m. exploring the open sky and counting stars. When we were together, you drove me to the farthest cloud conceivable.

And suddenly, there's too much of everything.

I can't tell anyone about the battle raging within my thoughts. My soul's bruises aren't ready to mend.

More than the moment I lost you, I'm suffering from the sorrow of losing myself.

Your love was my strength, but... Knowing it might also be my weakness numbed my senses and prevented me from becoming one of the most beautiful women.

Our memories will live on, even after we pass away.

You made my heart flutter with joy. And it is true that beautiful memories, not stuff, provide the nicest feelings in the world. We spent an irreplaceable, unforgettable, and immutable time together. And I'm willing to hold it close to my heart and carry it with me to the grave.

I wanted us to be stuck in a never-ending loop.

I am heartbroken.

But it's not simply that I've lost a partner; I know I'd never choose to move on instead of wishing things were different.

I wanted us to be together for the rest of our lives, forever and always.

My eyes yearn for more and more of you.

I'd like to immerse myself in you and feed off your kisses.

I recall you calling me right before going to bed to end the day with my voice, and I remember calling you shortly after waking up to begin my day with yours.

I'm curious to see how you're doing now that you're not with me. I'm curious to see if that Cheshire cat grin is still on your face. Even if we happen to pass each other on the street, I know we won't stop. But I'm certain I'll crack a grin.

In some way, everything reminds me of you.

Even if everything fades away, the person you were to me will live on in my heart for the rest of my life.

Certain places we used to visit still hold a special place in my heart. I'm still enchanted. Even if I attempt to ignore the feeling of belonging, it resets everything, every second we've spent together in that air.

Do you ever feel the urge for closure?

I wanted to know why the things that are happening in my life are happening in the first place.

To bring all of the pictures of "what if" scenarios to a close, I needed a conclusion.

I'm terrified. What if...

What if the sky falls in on me, the day I choose to be happy again by running into your arms?

Would you ask me to sacrifice myself for you again, if I located you someday and let the sky fall on me?

I want to be happy again, even if it's just for a second.

However, the notion of you and me sounds so much better in my head, and it seems so much more heart-breaking in reality.

Every day we spent together, you never ceased to astound me.

I'm not sure what I'd do without you.

At the very least, I know that even if I get you back, things will not be as easy as they were before.

But it's difficult to go through life knowing you're no longer a part of mine.

You deserve someone who believes you're too valuable to lose.

Perhaps you didn't feel butterflies in your stomach the last time you looked at me. You didn't intend to break my bones by jumping on them, did you?

Did you fall out of love?

Love, on the other hand, is something we do, not something we stumble into. So, how did you lose all of your feelings for me?

You know, I gave it my best for you. Wasn't that sufficient for you?

Perhaps someone else was providing you with something you were craving.

But you know what? Certain things are unavoidably irreversible.

There is no turning back once a line has been crossed.

I still love you. Yes, everyone may think I'm a moron, but I do.

And I believe it's acceptable to miss something intensely while still refusing to want it back. I'm afraid of the aspects of myself I don't comprehend.

And now I'm aware that the ones that mean the most to us will undoubtedly depart at some point.

So now I know, and my heart is no longer up for grabs. It's been difficult for me to heal and move on. I'm unable to reassemble the fragments of my heart.

State Of Bliss

by Harshvi Soni

Do you remember our first eye contact?
The nervous smile and the butterflies?
The way you smirked and walked away.

But did you know?
I waited for that day.

Did you look back after you walked ahead?
Did you know I was blushing hard, my cheeks turning red?
And those coincidental encounters were pure bliss,
Everything played in my mind when we had our first kiss.

Now you're lying by my side, fixing my hair,
Same old butterflies every time we stare,
Same old smile in the bed that we share,
The presence of you is so comforting,
All my insecurities seem to be vanishing.

I found peace in you when everything was so chaotic,
Now I can't even relate to Taylor's music.
And I know, when you go to sleep,
I hope you think about me.

Let's Meet Again

by Laveena Chandnani (Inking Hearts)

Let's meet again
Unexpectedly, unknowingly
Completely unknown to each other
And let's see if we can fall in love with each other again!

Let's meet again
To relive those moments
That background music filled of romanticism
The surroundings filled with the word "love"
Butterflies in our stomachs
And our eyes looking for each other in the crowd.

Let's meet again
Experience that first talk full of shyness and blushed smiles
That first eye contact where we craved to have each other
That first blushing smile and the first hug we had together

Let's meet again
Unexpectedly, unknowingly
To relive that moment
Where we held each other's hands
Promising a life full of love we gave to each other
Where we shared infinite laughter, memories and 3:00 a.m.
talks.

Let's meet again
To experience the fights we had together
The beautiful moments of togetherness
Where we shared hugs, cuddles, and kisses!

Let's meet again,
To know what "love" truly means
To know how hard and fulfilling long distance relationships are.
To know what happens when we crave to see someone and
they're in front of our eyes magically, saying "Surprise!"
And our eyes filled with tears of meeting someone after so long.

Love

by Laveena Chandnani (Inking Hearts)

A feeling that is the reason
For our sleepless nights
For our fantasising dreams
For the modification in ourselves
For the sake of the unknown.
That is love!

The reason
For waking up at twilight
For our daydreaming
The feeling that kills us
And then gives us the reason to live
That is love!

The reason

For the breaths that

One breathes wholly

The feeling

That melts in the eyes

That makes one hold their breath

That is never scared of anyone

That is immortal

That is interminable

That passes every second

That is love!

That Girl

by Tanushree Dewanjee (Elena)

It was the early morning of the thirteenth of December when I first saw her sitting in the very corner of the cafe with her usual order of double chocolate chip Frappuccino and her laptop. Usual, because after that day, I saw her every day on the same seat with the same order. She always looked outside and smiled at the falling snowflakes as if they were conversing with her. Her appearance was always as soft as herself, at least that's what it felt like. I always saw her in her signature outfit, a pink turtleneck hoodie, a white fluffy muffler around her neck, and a pink beanie with white platform-heeled boots. Oh no, I did not observe her like a science project. (Okay, maybe I did.) But it was amusing for me. Not everyone could pull off that outfit so beautifully as her, but somehow, her innocence and simplicity made her look attractive even in that simple attire.

The only thing that was rare about her were her eyes. Her right eye was blue, and her left eye was amber-coloured. What is this thing called again? Hetero – oh yeah, heterochromia. But her different eye colours didn't lessen her charm even a little bit, making her look more majestic every time.

Coming to the cafe every day at the same time became my habit. I was never a coffee person, but that day I came because my lack of sleep could affect my work. I never knew that coming into the cafe to ease my sleepiness would become my favourite part of the day. Now every day, I found myself sitting across her seat with a black coffee on my table and me stealing glances at her. Don't think of me as a creep because I never followed her outside the café, and she knew (or so I thought) that I was watching her, anyway, because she also looked up from her laptop and smiled at me sometimes. I never intended to make myself this desperate only to see her, but looking at her eyes, I could feel the warmth of spring even on those cold winter days.

It was that day when I had to go out of Washington for a day to meet my mother and I missed the chance to see her. For the whole day, her warm and soft eyes haunted me, and I couldn't help myself from imagining her face every time I saw a girl. I came back the next day to find myself again in the same place, but that day, she did something different than the other days. She looked at me, gave me her warm smile, and then scribbled something on a sticky note before sticking it under the table and walking out of the cafe, and of course, smiling at me on her way out. I walked to her table and pulled out the paper she stuck under the table.

"Where were you yesterday?" It read.

I grinned and immediately grabbed a pen from the barista to write a reply.

"I went out of Washington to visit my mother. Did you miss me yesterday?" I penned down.

I stuck the handwritten note in the exact place where she did. Then, I had no choice but to wait for her reply the next day.

The next day, she came early, and the first thing she did was to pick the note from where she had left it. She smiled fondly and looked at me, clearly happy by my reply, and again scribbled something on another note before sticking it. The rest of the hour went by her watching the snowflakes and me watching her. And when she left, I walked to her table to check her reply.

"Oh, that's good! Yes, I did miss you. The seat across from me was so empty without you," It read.

I don't have an idea why but knowing that she missed me gave me a strange kind of relief. The next days were spent like this. She wrote something on a sticky note, and I replied to it and then she asked something again the next day. We got quite close by talking to each other and Christmas passed like this.

"We've been talking for the last ten days but I still don't know your name." a note from her read.

She asked me this, two days before Christmas. Then I replied to her, "My name is Eric," in another note.

The next day, I saw her smiling after seeing the note and mouthing "Eric". I thought multiple times to gather enough courage and talk to her, but when the time came, I again decided that talking to her through notes was far better as she might not like me approaching her for a talk directly, and it might make me look desperate. I didn't want to mess up whatever we had between us.

It was the last day of 2021, and I was waiting to see her again. That day, she was wearing something different from her daily outfit. She was dressed in a wine-coloured dress with black tights, a white cardigan and high-wedge black heels. Her long, black hair was straight, not curled like every day and she wasn't wearing a beanie either. Even though she looked so good without makeup, that day she looked more mature than the other days with her smoky eyes and dark red lips. She took her order and sat in her fixed place. Her eyes adored the snowflakes like always but then she looked at me and something about her stare was unusual. Our gaze held for longer than usual and then she turned to her laptop. The rest of the hour she didn't look up, not even for once. But while going out she wrote the note and stuck it under the table and while walking past me, her hands lightly touched mine, and it felt like a goodbye gesture. For the rest of the day, I was left thinking about it, about why she did that all of a sudden. When her seat was empty, I walked to her seat and pulled out the sticky note she had left for me.

"You're looking good today. Blue is certainly your colour. By the way, Happy New Year in advance. It was so nice to know you in the New Year," It read.

Her note confused me a bit and I didn't think of leaving a note again but decided to talk to her the very next day and tell her everything – how I found her beautiful from the very first day and her wine-coloured dress left me astounded, how I loved the way she smiled at the snowfall, that I loved the way she held the back of her pen in between her lips while she couldn't figure out something, that I loved the way she scolded her laptop for the internet problem. I wanted to tell her that I loved her. I loved this simple, unnamed girl who had crept her way into my heart without taking my permission. I was sure to talk to her the next day; the first morning of the year could be my best one. All I had to do was to wait for the next morning.

The next day, there was no sign of her. I waited for a week, but she didn't come. I started waiting for her in the late hours. When I had enough of waiting, I finally went to the barista and asked about her.

"Excuse me; do you know where the girl from the corner seat is? She didn't come for the last one week. So, I was thinking if she's sick or something?" I asked.

The barista girl, whose name tag read Carol, smiled at me politely.

"Oh, you mean Sophie. Yeah, she left."

I gasped. "Left? To where?"

"To her hometown, London. She comes here every December to celebrate Christmas and New Year with her grandparents and then leaves on the first day of the New Year. She's a very polite girl, without any snarky remarks or rudeness. She always treats us like we're her family. We miss her for the whole year. Don't worry; you'll see her again next December."

With that, she left to her work, leaving me dumbfounded behind.

She left. She left the town. How was I going to tell her about my feelings? About my love for her? Would she return? The way Carol said, yes, she would. I knew she would. She had to, because she returned every year for her grandparents. Only this year, she would return for me, because she needed to know what I felt about her. I only had to wait for a year. Then, I'd tell her everything and make her a part of my life. Yes, the wait would be worth it, and she would be with me again.

Someday…

The Dread In Me

by Gauri Agarwal (Periwinkle)

I'm more afraid of
The time I will be gasping for air
My tears dissolving in the water around me
Slowly, I will close my eyes and fall asleep.

I'm more afraid of
The way it will hurt
Watching my blood ooze out
Then I will close my eyes and fall asleep.

I'm more afraid of
The feeling of falling down
I will hit the never-reaching ground
And I will close my eyes and fall asleep.

I'm more afraid of

The pain I will feel before dying

Than death itself

But it will all end

Because I will close my eyes and fall asleep.

Life Without You

by Sanaskriti Saha

Life without a friend
Is almost like clouds without rain
Life without you just wouldn't go right
And I won't be able to get through each day and night
When times are tough in my life here
It has brightened my days just knowing you care
You magnify my happiness when I'm glad
You help me heal my wound whenever I am sad
Being with you is just like accompanying the sea
Shores that touch me and I feel glee
When my world is full of lies
The truth is handed only through your eyes
Albeit you know I'm steady
But you're still ready
For if I fall sometime,
You give your back to keep as mine
For there are no goodbyes

Bonding stays cemented for miles
Knowing that you're always beside
And what your words describe
Every time giving me a surprise
And remembering that blissful moment when you smiled
The sun actually rose
Befriending with the pines
Tears pouring off those cheeks,
Also, after reading your letter a hundred times!

In His Arms

by Sanaskriti Saha

To my love, my father

Amidst the heavy crowd,

I was the only one who could

Discern clearly the adorned God.

I did see the people bowed

And looked small before God and me

While I was sitting in the arms of my dad.

When everyone was tensed crossing the busy road,

I was enjoying a video of a crazy toad.

Neither had I watched the right side,

Nor did I see the road being wide.

I never bothered about the traffic signal or horde,

As I was holding the hand of my hero dad.

The heavy fever and body aches

Couldn't make my heart shake.

Failure and fear never made me cry

And the evils and problems never even tried.
As the caress of my dad's hands on my forehead,
Accorded instant energy in my veins and I moved ahead.
In the midst of the loud wails of the mob,
Hearing the annoying songs on the radio,
Amid the blaring whistle of a train,
Ignoring the *chaiwala's** rhythmic chain,
I did have a pleasant sleep,
And in my dad's arms, I went so deep
No mobile, no watches, and no gadgets I bore.
All I carried was only a camera to adore,
As I had my dad beside me to cuddle
And I behaved like a cute toddler.
Kept me out of harm's way, his arm,
And I was the princess of his realm.

Annotations-
**Chaiwalas*: Tea-seller

The Boy At The Library Door

by Dr. Mansi Kothekar

It was the last class before recess and there was no sign of our teacher just when an announcement was made that he had called in sick and we'd be having a 'free period'. It was exciting news on a fairly mundane day in the life of a bunch of seventh graders. While some couldn't wait to hit the grounds, my best friend, who was also my benchmate, rushed to the library to catch our favourite spot by the window. She grabbed her Nancy Drew and I picked up my David Copperfield and continued reading from where I left my last literature lesson.

Some time into it and I was thirsty and had to go back to the classroom, which was the diagonally closest room to the library. I sipped some water down my throat and just while stepping out of the classroom, I saw a boy facing half his back, and his right profile in my direction standing at the library door giggling at some joke his friend had cracked, which now I could tell for sure must have been the silliest pun! But that day, I had seen the single, most beautiful smile in all thirteen years of my life. I remember the moment so vividly like it was yesterday.

Even today, when I open my school box, and all the memories rush, most of them run like a movie flashback in 2X. Except this moment is a slow, zoomed-in front shot, where even the glimpse of that 'giggle fading into a smile' lingers in front of my eyes as I see him pass by with his friend, completely unaware of my existence, as was I until that moment. But it wasn't going to take me till the end of the day to find out about him. Which it didn't. He was in the same grade, just a different section. And who was a complete stranger to me until a few moments ago, started getting familiar with every passing day.

Not realising what just hit me, I banged into a wall, lost in the beauty of a moment for the very first time in life, only to find my daydream was timed out and I rushed back to the library before anyone would notice my foolishness, which, at the time, was a romantic 'meet-cute' in my head. I went back to a questioning look on my friend's face, to which I just smiled and kept on smiling goofily from the corner of my mouth for the rest of the day.

This little romantic encounter of my feelings was so shushed that I didn't even confront myself for a year. Until one fine day, classes shuffled, and he was shifted to my section. And I got to see him a lot more… The more I observed him, the more he stood out. (Or at least I made him in my head). But there was something different about him from the rest of the class. From the innocence radiating through that face and a smile that lit up the world, he was a kid with a lot of allergies and would fall sick every now and then and bunked school most days, still managing to score well in academics, and loved football.

And I was living in a world of my own, reading books and watching romantic movies and before I knew it, I was already living in one. Not much later that year, Mr. Beautiful Smile and I became friends and shared the same group of friends. And this liking took a back seat as our bond grew stronger. I remember we fought a lot but also confided in each other. His hobbies and crushes would change every week and he would come and tell me all about how he found them unusual and interesting (like I found him). I used to be right there beside him and yet failed to draw his attention.

We were at a very impressionable age and our likings were changing with every passing day. Looking at the type of girls he liked, I figured I was not his type, as I wasn't so girly and didn't have straight hair (mine was wavy and frizzy and short), I couldn't sing, and I was ill-groomed and boyish. But I wrote poems even then, and I loved myself. However, just hearing him speak so highly of them, it became my life's mission to be like one of those girls and I started finding flaws in myself in the name of betterment. I was transforming into a different person, who even I wasn't very fond of.

And today, I only wish the mountains I climbed for him, the roads I walked bare-feet in the scorching sun burning my skin, if only I walked that path for myself, if only I had climbed that mountain for the fresh breeze on my face and so much more oxygen in my lungs, if only I had appreciated the beauty of nature while on that journey, if only I had taken that random stranger at that bookstore seriously, when out of nowhere he had called out, "Hey, you look beautiful." If only I had believed my family and friends when they told me how precious I was, and anybody who didn't appreciate me didn't know what he was losing. If only I hadn't moved cities for him, if only I knew no matter where I went, I'd never find him.

Because he didn't exist…

The little boy at the library I fell for, did exist though. Just that, the little boy had grown into a completely different human. Yes, he was my friend, but I didn't know who he had become. He was a man none of us knew. And I was chasing the most romanticised version of a very flawed human being. I was chasing my idea of love. I was chasing a fairy tale. And I thank my stars that love was unvoiced. I thank my stars I did not let 'that man' change my love for that innocent allergic kid with a red nose. The smile that spilled magic. That boy at the library door.

Illusion

by Tanisha Joshi (Freesia)

You're not a reflection of your soft-spoken love,
You're a phantom of deadly silence weeping beneath the
summer moon,
Death isn't the only way to disencumber your past,
You see, you don't care anymore.
Despair has carried you to forlornness
And you exceptionally urge for something sweet,
Hankering for a love that doesn't exist.
Your inner light swallowing all the darkness within you,
Embers guide you through your way,
An apocalypse tumultuously applauded.
For your lovelorn soul the world turned hollow,
You're a book full of calamities and debacles,
You don't have any author,
And this book is your fate anonymously written by you.
All your blood dripping down the chin,
All your scars bleeding,

All your bruised eyes brimming with tears,
All your love realised for years,
Wide, empty heart.
And can you feel the distance between you and your lover?
It's extended,
You start writing about her,
The feelings and the midnight cravings,
A portrait of her shade,
Not a hindrance,
Embracing the dark mind in the late and silent hours,
Mourning out loud because you know you've been hurt,
But you wish to get more.
Find a road for your sham love,
For your repetitive stories,
And for your monotonous rhymes,
Tired of repetition, retread.
Was it actually love or just an illusion?
You still doubt it
Because all your proposals turned into gravel
You find gratitude flooding your hands only because a person
has left,
And here you are, worn to your bones but my love you deserve
the blooming flowers,
The world not just yours but ours
But I cannot give you mine.

You, Me, Love, And Hope

by Tanisha Joshi (Freesia)

Yes,

I'll write about you,

I'll write about you until you realise that this love which
conjugates us is no more alive,

It's dead.

This love plumped down in the bottomless oceans.

Horizonless feelings,

Unfathomable sadness,

These scars which you gave me,

The good in your evil.

Everything you ever did to me,

Wounds, bruises, and my forever pounding heart,

But I learned the good in your evil.

My optimistic mind which helped me to learn from you.

Engendering positivity.

I forget to breathe sometimes,

And you know you can help, but you don't.

When I peep into my heart,

All I find is an isolated island.

Submerging,

Immeasurably flooding emotions,

I feel as if I'm already too empty to give myself anything now,
for all the love I had.

All I know, I'm worthless.

Because the love you need is the only love you can provide.

But I'll still write about you to reach you.

To give you the love you never gave me.

And every time they'll read my poetries,

They would fall for you.

I'll write about your crepuscular eyes,

Dimming, mellowing with every elapsing moment.

I'll make them fall for you,

To make you realise my heart has no love left for myself,

How can a heart love another when it doesn't love the self?

Look a little deeper, look a little harder,

There's still love within you.

Immense love which resides for you and you, alone.

And I'll continue writing till doomsday.

Can Liberation Be A Symbol Of Love?

by Ria Gandhi

When I'm engulfed in my own thoughts,

It leaves me pondering over society's definition of relationships,

friendships, and love.

My mind travels to the old mentalities and definitions,

That the society had laid generations back,

Out of which women was everyone's favourite topic.

A lot of things were expected out of a woman,

That must have made her resilient and a holistic learner.

But even after living up to such massive expectations,

She was not made to feel liberated.

Few generations later, away from the old mentalities,
Came an inevitable change,
Where some men and many women were ready to adapt to new
beliefs,
Where love is no longer equivalent to doing someone's laundry.

Today, love is probably doing the laundry together,
Being there for each other, yet not taking away each other's
liberation.
Not associating liberation with we will do what we want,
But making sure the decisions and steps we take are mutual.
Now, can we call liberation a symbol of love?

Beauty Isn't Skin Deep

by Nilesh Mandhyan (Neel)

We are all beautiful in our own way, not because of those filters or editing we have on social media today. We are not beautiful because of the clothes we choose to wear, or the makeup we wear. We don't appreciate ourselves because we haven't seen ourselves in those small happy moments when we are genuinely laughing at a joke a friend cracked, or when we are smiling at our loved ones, or when we are blushing. This is seen by others and thus appreciated by them. We don't see ourselves in those precious moments when we are expressing real emotions and not faking it for a picture. Those tiny happy moments show our actual beauty. You don't know how amazing you look when you smile or laugh or blush.

Nobody is too fat, or too slim. No complexion is too dark or too pale. No one is too short or too tall. Fat people are chubby and as cute as a teddy bear. Slim people are also pretty. People with a dark complexion or light complexion, both are beautiful. Short people look cute and so do tall people. These physical aspects don't define beauty. Beauty is those small tasks you complete every day, things that you do, and that happy look that you get when you are just simply living life to its fullest. Beauty is not how you look; it depends on who you are. It depends on not what brand you wear but how you present yourself in front of people. Everyone is beautiful; physical aspects of beauty aren't what beauty as a whole is; rather they are just a part of it. So, don't let your self-confidence burn to ashes if you have a few extra pounds in your body or you don't have the skin colour like the Instagram model you saw while scrolling through reels. Be you; be original because that is what matters.

"You are enough just as you are."
~Meghan Markle

Escape Is A Lie

by Nilesh Mandhyan (Neel)

Please don't be so shy
You and your eyes
Are always nearby.

I tried to deny
But I was always so high
I said I won't cry
But it's time to say goodbye.

"Please let me go!"
Go ahead and scream
"This ain't reality."
Baby, it's a dream.

Clothes of the royals
Blood on my tee
Soaked in the oil
Can somebody burn me?

Time flew like a river
You were my lifeboat
But no matter how hard I tried
I couldn't change the present.
Time is deadly
Time is like a maze
I can't find my way out.

I know all your secrets
I know all your lies
I know all your games
I see your disguise.

Blood on my tee,
I am a liar.
Can somebody burn me?

Dark energy enlivens me
Blood on my tee
Can somebody burn me?

Fading Corals Fading Friendships

by Tiara Mehrotra (Skye)

Water splashes all around,
I am gasping for air,
But I don't hear a sound.
Grizzled light subdued,
Just like a fading coral,
All I can hear is,
"Lost colour?"
"Yes, me too."

Hanging around my neck, an opal necklace,
Gifted by my friends.
Which once covered me,
With its aura of colours,
Just so perfectly before.
Now it has faded to a hoary nightmare.

I feel polluted,
I feel left behind,
There are hurricanes pouring in my mind.
Drowning in the water yet so dirty,
Barnacles achieving more,
Makes me want to question my sanctity.

The choking is getting stronger with every breath,
I'm panicking to be understood faster.
The more I try,
It sinks me further.
Now, all I feel is fear.

The water is seeping deeper,
Looking for signs,
In the aquamarine dressed horror,
Hoping for a sign,
But getting insane rather.

I scream as loud as I can,
But all I hear,
is my voice, so sore.
A spark catches my eye,
The opal turns red,
Things could not get clear anymore in my head.

My voice was my sign,
All I have to do is let go of something which was never mine.

I clasp my necklace and jerk it off,
The film reel it played, were scars after all.
I reach for nirvana,
Without thinking about the trauma,
The innocent girl,
Is now way stronger.

Just like a faded coral
All I want to hear is,
"We'll get past this."
"Trust me, will you?"

Forbidden Love

by Tiara Mehrotra (Skye)

Wanted to be Psyche, but
Ended up being Icarus.
The fine line between sacrifice,
And self-destruction became clear.
As I fell, even Poseidon bewailed
But
Apollo failed to show any apprehension.
It seemed like a sad prose,
As my wings burnt.
Teardrops shun,
At the sad spectacle.
But unlike the tragedy
Millennials celebrate me as
"The sun-kissed girl who fell
But in the hands of freedom."

It Takes Two

by Bhumika Khandelwal

"It takes two people to help you take a shit, what made you think that you are allowed to recite your opinion all just by yourself?"

Everyone stopped laughing when the doorbell rang.

It was the neighbours with a bowl full of brownies along with a smiling face and a wedding invitation.

The moon appeared full that night.

It takes two people to help you take a shit. Two people.

This single line kept repeating itself again and again while he was sitting next to the window, waiting for the clouds to go, so the moon could reappear.

He was waiting to look at the moon one more time and question him. Questions about the unfairness he had suffered and the pain he had been addicted to.

The clouds had started moving away from the moon again.

There, a crescent had just formed. But this time, it appeared red. Well, some call it "the beginning of the end". The very first step towards what's already been written. He kept staring at it with his neck tilted left and pale brown eyes.

"Move aside or you will lose everything."

"Move aside."

He started shaking as soon as he remembered this. He was sweating now and losing his breath slowly.

"MOVE ASIDE, YOU SHITFACE!"

Yes, that's what triggered him and made him fall out of his chair.

It all went quiet now, nothing made any sound.

The moon had lost its colour now. He finally cried.

Cried because he deserved to. Four years of patience and he was finally suffering.

Out of his chair, in his dark room with turquoise-coloured curtains wrapped around a pillar shined a moon with grace and sadness.

Oh no, did you not realise that the moon was not a happy child, and neither was he?

Because years ago, he denied moving aside when he was asked to.

It was his second marathon, and he was all about to win it until someone made him fall.

No, he didn't just lose the race. He lost his energy to fight, to run anymore.

It's almost unbelievable how someone's actions affect us to our very core, and we never allow ourselves to realise it.

After all, it took him four years to realise that he had lost control over everything he did.

But the question here isn't about when you realise it; it's about when you finally accept it.

The fact that giving up on some fights in life is too peaceful to have it destroyed by the urge to always win.

And by the way he wasn't hopeless, just paralysed.

An Ode To Seasons

by Mansi Valera

2:00 a.m.

It's midnight

Fog covering your house

And loneliness, your soul.

You scroll through hundreds of contacts

But end up calling no one

How could you know?

The next day you wake up feeling lonelier.

10:00 a.m.

Sunshine in sight

Coffee in your hands

Your soul caffeinated

You feel like telling someone how good the weather is

And how the skies are just perfect blue

But you end up penning it down in your diary.

3:00 p.m.
You watch the rain pouring from your window
Filled with cracks and stains
You think about how you should not think about broken
friendships and long-lost people.

You curl up in a blanket
It feels like some warmth is there
After an eternity
You hold your favourite book
And go to sleep without realising.

You go on long walks in autumn
So long that it hurts your feet
You sleep without overthinking that night.

You are so careful with fallen leaves
Because you consider yourself one.

While cooking, reading, and listening to your favourite band
Just for a second, you wish for someone
To be there with you
A friend or maybe a soul who gets you like no one else does.

You watch people hanging out
You feel sad
Friends come to your rescue
So, you sit there, watching F.R.I.E.N.D.S.
With a tub of chocolate ice cream in your hands

Your brain might freeze from that ice cream
But your heart feels warm
You find your solace.
Finally!

How could you know?
The next day you wake up feeling
A little less than more.

The Love I Have Been Waiting For

by Muskan Sahani (Laughwithsmiley)

The love I've been waiting for.

It's been years and years of searching, being solitary and merrier
with the passing time, reaching the point where the nods were
about to end in the hope it might be held.

Drawing the silhouettes, on a canvas filled with love.
I painted him, a little dark, a little blurred.

So different from the canvas I painted, far from the darkness,
I saw him limpid.
A lucid thinker and man with full charms.
So unexpected and real.

Skilfully drawn, with love and forgiveness,
An advisor and a lover.

I carried my life with the inspiration of Poseidon,
Sometimes filled with rage, and disruptive,
I was a fan of Nyx,
Also had different Pandora boxes along my side.

But he is never afraid,
Instead, falling asleep along my side is still his favourite choice.
His voice is like a melody playing inside me, songs of love.
Throwing the lights of hope and making me believe in the Elpis.

I believe in love
I believe in him.

Falling in love selflessly, sprinkles of truth, joy in every touch.
Forming the constellations of moments and rain of romance.

Promises to keep, love shall be nourished

Is anything better than the canvas filled with colours of love by
us?

My Monster

by Veena Antony (Drizzling Lover)

Maple leaves,
Orange pumpkins,
No knowledge of the West,
I sailed from the East,
Through the neighbour's window,
Everyday two hazel eyes,
Peeked around my home.

My first Halloween,
Oh god, I am alone,
Haunted thoughts,
Scary, dark nights,
The sound of crickets,
I'm eager to sleep,
But my eyes, they resist to close.

My mind was not clear.
I was scared.
Never felt this much fear.
Suddenly, a knock
The door opened by me,
Echo of the monster startled me,
Rest is history.

A monster owns me now,
Owner of those hazel eyes,
In the next life also,
Surely, I want to fall into those arms.
True, I cannot leave the West now,
Everything changed, cause' I'm in love,
A handsome, loving monster captured me forever.

Why Crows Hate Rice Balls

by Veena Antony (Drizzling Lover)

Present

"Sid, please forgive me. It's been ten years. Please don't kill me like this. Come."

Tears roll down from my eyes as I look at the sky. This is the tenth year that the crows have ignored my offerings.

I am Brad from Las Vegas. Eleven years ago; the love of my life Sidharth (Sid) and I had visited the Grand Canyon, Arizona. It's one of the seven wonders of the world. Then, the Grand Canyon and Colorado River witnessed a day which I cannot erase from my memory, even if I die.

Eleven Years Ago

It was Sid's father's fifth death anniversary. Every year, on the same day, we visited the Grand Canyon. Sid was doing it as per the wish of his father. He was the only son of his parents. He was from Kerala, India. But they were settled in Las Vegas. We had been classmates since we were in school. Sid was a very reserved person. He usually remained quiet. He was a prodigy at school and due to his looks and grades, all girls used to hover around him. Although he never had a crush on anyone, he had been my crush since we were fourteen. I had no courage to confess this to him because I knew he was from a very conservative background which wouldn't have accepted our love. In their family, only arranged marriages happened. They never accepted love marriages; so, how could we expect them to accept homosexual love?

On the death day of Sid's father, I saw some rituals done by Sid for his him. Everything was new for me as I had never seen such rituals been done. On the sixteenth day of his demise, they had done some poojas* near the bank of a river. Sid later explained the belief behind those rituals. I couldn't believe it. I felt as if it was a silly childhood thing. A tantrik* chanted a few mantras. Sid was wearing a red dress; the tantrik put a rice ball on a banana leaf, and sprinkled black sesame seeds, basil leaves and flowers on it. Sid carried these things to the river, and three times, he sank in the water with those balls on his head. He placed the rice ball having sesame seeds in a place, then clapped his wet hands. A crow came and ate a part of it. Every year on his father's death anniversary, we'd come to the Grand Canyon with these rice balls. Usually, this ritual should be done at the bank of any river or sea, but Sid would do it on the Grand Canyon.

That was another story…

When he was in school, Sid visited the Grand Canyon with his parents. That was the first time he saw many giant black crows. He called it the "Grand Canyon Crow."

Then his father told him, "Sid, you are my only son and heir. After my death, I have only you to perform my liberation rituals. You shouldn't go to just any river. You have to come to the Grand Canyon for as long as possible. The Colorado River is here. When you offer rice balls and sesame seeds to me, I will come from the depth of Colorado, which is more than thousands of feet down to the Grand Canyon. I will eat the rice ball and will look at you then I will fly away with the flowers you offer. It will mean that I love you a lot."

Though it was not the full custom, after Sid's father's death, Sid followed his father's wish.

He told me the actual custom and ritual of their culture. In Kerala, only Hindus followed these rituals for departed ancestors. There would be a special day for the departed souls. Sid was a Hindu. Hindus would perform this ritual on 'Karkkidaka vavu*'. On that day of Karkidakam*, everyone would perform Bali* for their deceased ancestors. People would gather on riverbanks and beaches to offer this. They believed that departed souls attained moksha* if the rituals were properly performed that day.

At the time of death, one's sons had the duty to perform this Bali*. Every year, on the death anniversary, irrespective of gender, all children of deceased and blood relatives could do it. If no one exists, a loved one could. But elders wouldn't do it for younger ones. It was considered a sin of the living person. But if still no younger one existed, elders could do it. Sid lost his mother too, so he had to do it for her, too.

The rice balls and sesame seeds are offerings for souls. When the person clapped with wet hands, a crow was expected to come and eat a rice ball. Not all the crows, though. It had to be of a special type. Fully black without any grey rings, called 'balikaakka'. They were similar to Grand Canyon crows, but smaller in size. If a crow didn't come to eat a rice ball, it would mean that the soul was not satisfied, or the soul had a problem in attaining liberation, or it could be a feeling of unforgiveness or hate towards the person who was performing the ritual.

When we came for the last time, I was depressed, because Sid said that his family was looking for a bride for him. The next day, he was going to meet her for the first time. He seemed to have no problem with that. But all I could think about was that I would lose him. I had no choice left but to make a confession. I wanted to know the truth. If he, too, had similar feelings, it would be a huge win for me. If he accepted that girl next day, I wouldn't get a chance later. I hoped he, too, was in love with me. Whether his answer was a yes or no, I wanted to end my suffering. So, I decided to confess.

He finished the rituals for his father. He looked so calm. I thought it was a special day for him and he was in a good mood, so he would be able to think properly. We went to the skywalk and came back to the Eagle Point, and then I caught hold of his hand and confessed that I loved him dearly. I kissed him too. He was shocked. He started shivering and pushed me away. He looked at me in disbelief and started panting. We were standing just a few meters away from the edge. Sid looked at me strangely, and unconsciously, started moving towards the edge. The watchman who saw us came running, but he was too late. He had touched the edge. I couldn't get hold of him, and in front of my eyes, he fell down to the depths of the Canyon, into the hands of the Colorado River. I wanted to jump along with him, but the watchman held me tightly.

Present

I lost him forever. The guilt and loss haunt me every day. Today is his tenth death anniversary. Every year, I visit the Grand Canyon on this day. It is Sid's father's death anniversary, too. For both of them, I come here with rice balls, sesame seeds, basil leaves, and flowers. For my Sid, I would place a red rose as a flower. I would clap my wet hands to invite the crow. But for Sid, no crow ever came. For his father, the crow would accept my offerings. But my Sid never accepted mine. I tried different foods to test the crows. They would eat sandwiches or any other food, but surprisingly they never accepted my rice balls. Yes, now I believe in souls. Sid and his father have no blood relatives in the US. His mother, too, passed away. I am the one who loves them the most. Even though Sid didn't accept me, they are my loved ones. So, I follow these rituals every year for them.

Every year I cry. I beg Sid's soul to forgive me. But I never gave up on my love. I am still single. I am still living for Sid. I don't want any other love in my life. Because of me, he lost his life. Until I get his forgiveness, how can I live peacefully? Because of me, I lost my love. He didn't get a chance to say a 'yes' or 'no' to my proposal. Without knowing it, how can I fall in love with another person? If Sid loves me, what will I do? Or why should I need another love? Sid's memory is enough for me to live.

"Sid, do the souls have a gender? Is homosexual love a crime? Can you hear me? I will never tell you to forgive me for your death, because even if you forgive me, I cannot forgive myself. But please forgive me for my confession. I selected the wrong place for the confession and the proposal. I could do it anywhere safe on the earth. Why did I say it on the edge of this dangerous Canyon? I am really sorry Sid. I was desperate. I was in fear of losing you. I became insane. I thought it was a special day. But it proved as a special day for me as it was special for you. Please accept my offerings, Sid. If you don't love me, if you hate me this much, why should I come here? If you don't accept my offerings, I will think you hate me the most. So next year onwards, I won't come. If you love me, come, and accept my offerings. Then, I am ready to come here to see you every week. Please, Sid, please." I cry. Offerings given to his father's soul are emptied by the crow; still, no crow has come for Sid.

I move to the edge of the Canyon from where I had lost my Sid. In a fraction of second, a crazy thought comes across my mind. "Shall I come to see you there, Sid? Do you love me? Say 'Yes' or 'No' to my face. I want to see you. Shall I jump, Sid? Can you forgive me, then?"

Suddenly, I hear Sid's voice. "Brad, no."

At first, I think I was hallucinating, but when I look around, no one is there. After eleven years, I am still able to hear Sid and recognise his voice. A guide standing far from me is explaining something to the tourists.

Then, I see a giant crow coming out of the Canyon as a rising sun from the depth of Colorado.

It is flying towards me. He encircles me once and sits near to the rice ball and eats it fully. He looks at me, takes my red rose in its beak and flies back to the depth of the Great Canyon.

"Oh, God! What was that? I can't believe it. He loves me. It is a yes!" I exclaim and look into the water with tears of happiness rolling down from my eyes.

"Sid, I love you too," I whisper to the water and leave the place with a smile.

Annotations-

Poojas: Prayers

Karkidakka Vavu-Karkidaka Vavu or *'Karkidaka Vavu Bali'* is a set of Hindu rituals performed on a specific monsoon day in the state of Kerala, India by adherents for their deceased ancestors. On the day of vavu or Amavasi people gather on the riverbanks and beaches to offer Bali

Karkidakkam-Karkidakam is the last month of the Malayalam calendar. (Malayalam)

bali: rituals (Malayalam)

Moksha: liberation (Sanskrit)

The Was

by Sandhita Agarwal

He seeps in through the memories into my skin
Like soaking in the rain on a wet, rainy day
Regrets of what was and what could have been
Of things that could have been done the other way.

A girl called gorgeous, a love so tender
Like music and lyrics dancing together
Alas! She was meant to stray yonder
A love so sullied left 'em effaced forever.

Climb up the steps of the ladder of time
See the crimes, the sins, and the regrets of thine
Clearer are the faces of people left behind
Their macabre visages burned into the mind.

They are happy, they are blessed
In a world that I could never own
I am haunted, I am cursed, and I am the unknown
And I sit here, waiting on my shattered throne.

Am I Not Good Enough?

by C. Dave

I am counting the stars

While you lie beside me on the green grass.

You snuggle your head deeper in my chest

While I wrap my arm around you.

Tighter.

I really wish that this moment doesn't end

'cause I know that living can't get any better.

I am smoking on the balcony

While I blow my smoke out, a smile creeps onto my lips,
remembering that day.

You asked me to break up with you if you weren't good enough
for me.

Without thinking twice, I placed my lips on yours.

Oh, how do I tell you that you are more than enough for me?

But right now, I am just penning this down in my diary.

While my brain makes its way back to the present.

A cigarette flicked between my fingers.

Sitting on the green grass, I look up to your window, admiring your petite figure.

So delicate and small.

I wish all of this were true.

But I know that I am not good enough for you.

Love Equation

by Shubhang Sharma

Love doesn't need the charm of alphabets,
Eternity falls for you, the devoted duet.

Enchanting eyes stimulates the deep-down love,
Grandeur gesture of fingers, unfolds the mystery of love.

Unspoken love holds the ladder of credence,
Crystals of ardour vocalise the love essence.

Lurking in the shadow of denial won't reveal you're smitten,
Unmasking your ethereal love will haul you from the valley of
love hidden.

Imperishable desire for love will coalesce the eternal soul,
It will define the authentic relation over vintage scroll.

Love, shower light on ominous silence of life,
Answering the deep down void with halcyon life.

Droplets of tears speaks enough to showcase emotions,
Summate expressions for the love-oceans.

May love be like wisteria's aroma,
An incarnation of seraphic adoration,
Granting life to the book of love-equation.

That Feeling Of First Love

by Sumedha Pant

First love is not only a feeling which makes you feel elated, but it stays inside you forever, like a carving etched on a stone. You can't forget that first feeling of holding each other's hand, smiling like idiots when you went home after meeting for the first time and doing random things that usually do not make sense. First love is like a breath of fresh air that will make you feel relaxed and at the same time, it will blow your mind. First love is quite sophisticated. You have to handle it with patience, because the moment you are careless, it will lose its smooth phase and you will end up with bumps which will be difficult to get over.

That feeling of staying with each other forever and seeing each other every second is amazing, and when it does not happen the way you want it, you crave for it more and more. You can be each other's armour, the happy place, and much more.

First love is so happening that when it arrives, you just get goosebumps even thinking about it. You want to cross every boundary which you have made earlier just for being with that one person whom you consider your everything right now.

First love makes you do stupid things sometimes, like waiting for hours just to see your person or just finding different ways to talk to them while you are doing something else, keeping in mind that you want that person to be yours only, forever, and ever. First love gives you the strength to fight every problem of yours and achieve what you want. It gives you a reason to be with someone and have them by your side every time you fail or pass in life.

First love can never be explained, because both of you have achieved the success of staying with each other and everyone knows your story, or the love has left you shattered, and you can't just express what it was like. The harmony which first love creates is just magical with a lot of emotions. You just have to feel it carefully, because this harmony is not loud enough to make you hear it.

First love is also like a piece of art which you have to understand with all the efforts you can make. Some of us don't believe in all of this, we just say love doesn't exist, but it does, it's just that love waits for the right time to come in front of us and let us experience it.

Growing together with each other is an ice walk but growing apart from each other and still being with each other asks for lots of courage, patience, and strength. And when you succeed, you will be the luckiest and happiest one and you will be proud of yourselves.

The journey of being someone's first love and making them yours is tough, but when it happens, you'll be the happiest person. The person with whom you have seen billions of dreams will be yours till eternity, and it will be the beginning of a life you'd have always wanted.

First love is just magical...

Rainwashed Muse

by Namoe

I walk through an incandescent membrane
Into a world of streets awash in rain and neon
Frozen thoughts crystallise in my mind
The sharp lattice piercing the heart's terrain
A spade through damp earth.

I've seen her before
On cloudier days
Aquatic eyes frantically searching for blue
Won't dress in sunshine
For fear of the darkness she knew.

I see her now
Lips dressed in red
Inspired by blood and a hint of cherry
Auroric eyes a new shade of nebulous
With alpenglow across her cheeks,

The rosy fingertips of dawn
Upon an Epicurean exodus.

Until I'm back again
In the world of streets
Awash in rain and neon
A tattered umbrella on cracked concrete.
Outside of the Irish Pub around the corner
Entrancing you are
Aglow in your storm
Of suits, smoke, and drizzle
With the same eyes
Under different clouds
Frantically searching for blue.

Words Of Love

by Bedavalli Misra

My eyes seek you in this mirage of dreams,
Whilst my lovelorn heart awaits the words
That shall herald your arrival,

I adorn the vanity, the capricious,
Indulge in the whims and fancies,
Oh, if you knew how I yearn for you, my love!
Would you hasten your footsteps, verily?

Would you embrace and twirl this being?
In this maze of words, yet again?
Presume that I need to soar yonder, in Utopia?
Assume that I am bound by these shackles?

Dare I trust your softly spoken words of love?
Let your heart wipe the ache within mine?
Thoughts unhindered, cease as you gaze at me,
Whirling and swirling, lost in a rhythm unknown.

Your whispered words of love reverberate.
I drown, yet again, in your world of words,
A world that intoxicates and bewitches.

Yonder, I see you singing a song of love, so sweet...
Lost I am, swaying to the music within,
As the crescendo peaks, I swirl away bewildered.
"Oh, Sema, dancer of mine!" You entreat with a smile,
"Cease this eternal duel and become mine."

Holding out a hand, you say, "Sing with me, my love,"
So, we sing a song like no other, a song about you and me,
Words of love, your heart has taught mine,
A love that has no beginning and no end...

Papa

by Rakhee Daryanani

Dedicating this poem to the first hero of my life,
the one who has been my pillar of strength and
the one who has loved me without boundaries: my Papa.

I came into this world and found myself in the arms of a man
My tiny palm was held by someone warm and strong
I held on with complete trust, knowing I won't be harmed
Because it was my first hero who held me with all his love
My Papa.

I was taken home and looked after with utmost care
Received everything that was for the best of me
The drop offs to school and pickups later on
My hero did all without any questions or expectations,

From tying my shoes to getting me popcorn.
He stood daily in the balcony till my school transport arrived
He never complained about all the expensive textbooks
Because he knew it was to build my foundation strong

To all the parent teacher meetings, he made his attendance
And made sure I was given the best education
Many a time he stayed with me at multiple sports sessions
Ignoring his work so that my work was completed.

He never stressed me to be the best
But to be a human being that made him proud
He supported me in the career that I chose
Where many would feel that career can be forgotten.

I made him proud with my career achievements
He was happy that I was happy
But one day came that I had to leave him home
To settle in my life far away.

He misses me and I miss him. too
But he knows that I will never forget him
My one and only hero who will never hurt me
The superman of my life, my wonderful Papa
I love you, Papa
See you soon.

That First Crush

by Sumedha Pant

I saw him for the first time standing in front of me, a well-dressed man who caught my eyes. The feeling of having a crush was so exhilarating. I used to see him every day, and out of nowhere, I was just finding reasons to talk to him. Days passed, and finally, I got the chance to talk to him, and then the journey of talking to my first crush began…

With time, we got to know each other very well, every single detail of what he liked and what he didn't. We started spending time with each other, sometimes at a chai tapri* or in the canteen.

Things were going well as I had gotten closer to my crush. The random smile I got while seeing him and even thinking about him was somewhat different. And acting insanely in front of him sometimes is what I enjoyed the most. Time flew and my feelings got stronger than before, but I knew that my crush would be a crush and nothing more than that, because the first crush is always special, and maybe we were never meant to be together. We are still with each other, not like a relationship but in an indescribable bond, cherishing every single moment, and having him as my first crush was an amazing feeling for me.

Seeing each other from a distance and then passing away with a smile is what makes my day perfect. I can't resist my urge to be around him and listen to him talking for hours. He is someone who can make me smile out of nowhere, whenever I feel a little low. He knows what is bothering me without letting me explain, and then gives the solution. We have had each other's back every single time, and no matter what, we ensure each other that everything will be alright in the end. Sometimes we fight, we argue, and we just don't talk to each other for a day, but then there's a feeling of missing each other in a very different way.

He is just perfect as a secret keeper, as a friend and more than that too; people say we are like Tom and Jerry, because whatever happens, we stay together.

I can see that the bond is getting stronger day by day, but the feeling of losing each other and growing apart is also nearing. This feeling never feels good because I have no idea whether I will see him again or not and if we will be able to reconnect the same way after such a long time. This feeling is weird, too, because again, I am unsure of what is going to happen further in life as this he-is-my-crush journey is going to end soon. All I am sure about is that he will be doing great in his life, and I will continue to annoy him by calling him names and teasing him. I know that this crush will forever remain a crush, as I will never ruin this friendship by telling him that I have fallen for him. Just thinking about expressing my feelings gives me a tingling sensation down my spine; if he reads this sometime later, I hope he gets what I could never tell him.

Annotations-

**chai tapri* – tea stall

A Letter To My Inspiration

by Vaneeta Chugh (Quing VC)

Dear inspiration,
You ignited in me a besire* to write,
Well, it started out with a howl,
Of wrecked me and my bruised soul,
I have got my heart broken.
But
Instead of wallowing in self-pity,
Sinking in sorrow like the rest,
I forced myself to surge upward,
And bring me to the world's heed.

You healed my wounded spirits,
With your torrid inferno of faith,
Uplifting me every time I fall down,
A crown of queen perched on my head.
You kept scribbling through thick and thin,
Never once getting tired of my crumbled failures.

I am grateful to you always and forever,
You stood by me when my heart went out,
You kindled a candle with light and way,
In the cavern, inked* in slaughter and slay,
Thank you, my spell-bounding pearly quill,
I crafted a wonderland of magicues* with you.

Annotations:
Besire – burning desire
Inked – coloured/soaked
Magicues – magical hues

The Humble Heart

by Vaneeta Chugh (Quing VC)

You gave me a little love,
Saying ias* more than enough.
But a single drop in drought,
Is an abundant source, though.
I would never cry and beg,
For you to love me and have,
A cavern chest carved in ice,
With naught but forlorn fuzzy
Viperous veins and litany lies
Yet your soul must be mine,
With your heart, shall I survive,
And I pray to Lord all along,
To make your heart swell and strong,
With warmth, steel will and sunshine,
Because
In every blimmery* blessing you pour,
Lord grants you a piece of yours.

Annotations-

**ias* - it was

**Blimmery* - Blooming Glimmer

Enigma Of Love

by Vaneeta Chugh (Quing VC)

Under the moon, in your arms,
My heart exploded in frenzy,
An enigma to be ruined by ashes,
You are, oh my dear love.
I felt a shudder in my arteries, baby,
When you transpired throughout,
My untethered soul,
Is it even mine to call?
No! Not at all!
All yours, my darling,
All yours!
I am all yours,
Inch by inch,
Blood by blood,
You sedated deep,
Within the core of
My being!

The Unopened Letter

by Priya Debnath (Priyal)

Anastasia

My life had been a total lie since the day I was born. The family, with which I spent my whole childhood, wasn't my family. Katherine, the sister who was born in front of my eyes, wasn't my sister. The person I loved with all my heart also turned out to be a liar. His name was Kevin, and what a handsome boy he was! He was the only boy in my life who was able to make my heart flutter like a new-born butterfly. I did everything I could with my power for him. He promised to keep me safe and protect my heart. He promised to love me with all he had, and he promised to marry me someday. He asked me to stay with him in his apartment, wishing to have me as close to him as he was able to. And to help Katherine's modelling career by taking her identity, since she was my responsibility. Yes, she was. Her looks were not enough to become a model and I loved my sister too much to leave her with disappointment. So, I added another lie in my life as a mask of my sister's face for the sake of him. Both of us did this for our loved ones. The only difference is, he was my love, and my sister was his.

Oh, how I wished that it was me who was in his embrace instead of Katherine when I found them in our apartment. Their bodies moulded with each other, making them one. Oh, how I hated the tears that left my eyes. The happiness of winning my first award ever vanished in a millisecond. It wasn't mine; it also belonged to her name, like the other things in my life. I was just a base of her success, just a face behind a mask. What an unfortunate I, in a fraction of a second. Kevin's eyes met mine and he stood up, wrapping the white cover around his naked form, making me look away in disgust.

"There you are, Anastasia. Come, have a seat. How was the award show? Sorry, I wasn't able to attend it, as you can see, I was busy with a very important meeting."

His words didn't have the fear of getting caught or any hope of explaining. It was full of mockery, which made me glare at him with full disgust and then at Katherine, who shamelessly laid there, covering herself only in a white satin sheet.

"Here, take your award, Katherine. And for heaven's sake, spare me. I'm done with all your games and tricks. I'm not going to be your face anymore." And that was the last thing I said before storming out of the apartment and their lives, for forever. And the last thing I remember was passing out at the bar while talking to a stranger beside me.

****

Headache rang in my head for the last hour. I could tell it was a hangover by the way my eyes saw things a little more deeply than usual. The only things which caught my eyes were a white bedroom and a white ceiling fan with gold plating on it. I hope I didn't do anything reckless in my drunken state last night, did I? I peeked inside the cover and find myself only in a white t-shirt and garments. Dang! What did I do last night?

"Don't worry. You're still a virgin – if you were one in the first place." My eyes turned to find the owner of the voice, and I witnessed a handsome well-built guy standing by the door. Very slowly, he came and sat on the bed beside me.

"Miss Williams, are you feeling okay? Or is your hangover causing you a problem?" He spoke in a low voice, and I couldn't help but admire how deep his voice was.

"Y-yeah. Yeah, I'm fine. But who are –" He cut me off before I could complete my sentence by giving me a glass of orange juice he was holding, gesturing me to drink and I slowly took a sip.

"I'm Cedric Smith. CEO of Smith & CO... Well, I know it's not an appropriate time to mention this, but again, I don't have much time for it. So, the girl who was set to marry me ran away with someone else. The preparation of marriage is almost done. And I want you to be my bride." He blurted all out without a pause. And less gracefully than a billionaire's wife, I spit the juice back in my glass and choked hard on it. He patted my back, waiting for me to calm down.

"You want me to do what?" was the only thing I managed to blurt out as I took myself down from the state of seeing black.

"I want you to be my bride. Look, Katherine, you're a well-known model, and I'm one of the richest bachelors of Washington. We can do this together and who knows, maybe after marriage, your career will take a new turn?" He spoke with hopelessness in his voice.

And did he just call me Katherine? Oh, so I didn't blurt anything out in my drunken state. Thanks to the heavens. But he was right; I didn't have anything to lose in my life, anyway. So, I could just take the chance. Who knew what life was bringing for me?

****

Everything just happened too fast in my life. It felt like yesterday that I caught Kevin with Katherine. But I knew very well that only a week had passed after that. And it had been a few days now that I was officially Mrs. Smith. Mrs. Anastasia Smith. But for Cedric, it was Katherine. I couldn't gather the courage to confess him my identity. Oh, Ana, why didn't you tell him in the first place? Why are you always so stupid?

"Mrs. Smith! Katherine!" The voice of Cedric pulled me out of my daze, and I found myself sitting by the window all by myself.

"Are you okay?" His voice was laced with concern, and I nodded.

"Well, I'm here to inform you about the party tonight. It's for your introduction to everyone. I hope you won't mind?" He spoke in a whispering tone, as if not sure what to say. I ran my fingers through my hair and looked at him, smiling.

"I'll be ready," I said.

****

I glanced at myself in the mirror for the last time. The dress was selected by Cedric. It was a red, sleeveless dress with a slit till the left thigh and had a small triangular shape cut on the stomach area. With a beach weave hairstyle and all red jewellery and lipstick, I looked like someone had just dipped me in blood. What was with Cedric and his obsession with red? Sighing, I looked at the letter I wrote for him revealing everything about my life. I couldn't do this. I couldn't add another lie in my life and drag Cedric in it, too. I took a deep breath and walked out of the room.

Guests were filling in the hallway. All I had to do was place the letter where he could find it and leave the house. Marrying him was the biggest mistake of mine in the first place. Now, I dragged him into my life of lies. But I had to make everything okay before it was too late. I took the stairs, careful enough that no one recognised me in the crowd, and suddenly, faced a bump with a hard chest in front of me. Looking up, my lungs dried. It was Kevin, with Katherine. Why on the earth were they here?

"Looks like our Ana tricked someone else into her trap of innocence. I must say, Ana, you trapped a billionaire, that's a big hand."

Tears well up in my eyes by the venom of my sister's, no, Katherine's words. I knew it; since she was here, she would destroy my chance to clarify everything. But not this time. I couldn't let her ruin Cedric's life by humiliating him in front of everyone. He had nothing to do with it. So, without any reply, I decided to leave the mansion. I could give him the letter later. But now, I didn't have enough energy to stay here and face these two poisonous snakes in my life. As soon as I reached the main door, a voice boomed, silencing everyone and stopping me midway.

"Ana!" It was Cedric. He just called me Ana. I turned around to look at his smiling figure.

"Ladies and gentlemen, if I have your kind attention, then I would like to tell you a story." He walked close to me, taking my hand in his, and began.

****

Cedric

"Do you need something else, Mr. Smith?" A waitress asked me, taking me out of the daze I was in. I pinched my forehead and looked up at her.

"No, I'm fine," I said. She nodded her head and left the VIP area I was in, and my eyes caught a glimpse of a half-drunk figure. I knew this person. Where did I see her? Oh, she was Katherine, the famous model. But why was she alone? And the moment I realised my steps, I was in front of her. She was oblivious of my presence, mumbling in her own fantasy world.

"Two Bloody Marys, please." She looked up at me, shocked by my sudden presence beside her but successfully hid it with her sheepish grin.

"Hello, Miss Katherine, I'm Cedric Smith." Her sheepish grin disappeared, and she blinked for a second, before laughing out loud, confusing me.

"You also think I'm Katherine. Wow, I must be a very good actress." She paused to bring the beer to her lips, and I replaced it with the drink that the bartender had just served us.

"Don't you think you're being a little too touchy, Mr. Smith?" A smug smirk set on her lips, making me chuckle.

"Just drink it, Katherine."

"Ana."

"What?"

"I'm not Katherine. I'm Ana, Anastasia. Her elder sister. Well, not particularly."

She sipped the drink casually, without looking at me. She was wasted. I could tell by the slurry words leaving her lips, but I couldn't help my curiosity.

"What do you mean by 'not particularly', Ana?"

Finally, she turned her whole body towards me and took a deep breath, as if trying to let out her deepest and darkest secret.

"I'm Ana. Anastasia Williams. Elder daughter of Mr. Joseph Williams. At least that's what I thought I was until I was eleven, eavesdropping on my parents talking about my adoption. Katherine Williams, whom people know is me, is my younger sister. Biologically or not. Kevin, the boy I loved with heaven and hell, played a trick on me, made me Katherine Williams, and then boom! I discovered them together on the bed today. What a great present for my success, isn't it? But I'm done now; I won't be

Katherine Williams anymore. I'm me. I'm Anastasia Williams. I left everything behind to move on with my life. Because I can. I'm strong enough to do it. But I won't tell anyone about her dirty little secret. Nope. I'll just disappear, like vapour. I know you're thinking of me like a poor victim. But I don't want your pity, thank you! I don't want anything from anyone. Nothing." And that was it. She passed out with her slurring words, making it hard for me to suppress my giggle.

Anastasia

"So here she is. Anastasia Smith. And the Katherine Williams she was pretending to be is standing there, with her boyfriend." Everyone's eyes turned to look at them, and they stood there, heads hanging low.

Holy! He knew everything about me and still decided to marry me! Why? He must be able to read my mind, as he turned at me and tilted my chin, making me look into his eyes.

"I know how you were feeling. Because the girl I loved was in love with my best friend. So, I know the feeling. I apologise to urge you in the sudden marriage as she confronted me at the last moment, and I didn't have any idea what to do with my broken heart. But I do hope that we could give each other a chance to explore love in each other and start a new life together. Is it okay with you?" His eyes gazed into mine, and for a second, I was lost in them. It took me a moment to find myself back and smile at him.

"Yes, I will. Mr. Smith."

"Call me Cedric.

"But-"

"Just call me Cedric, Ana."

"Cedric."

He smiled as if I had given him the whole world by calling him by his name, and pulled me closer to him, making me blush.

"I love you, Mrs. Anastasia Smith."

"I love you more, Mr. Cedric."

And who knew that my previous heartbreak was going to be worth it!

I Am Not A Stranger

by Vaneeta Chugh (Quing VC)

Don't walk upon me, dear!
For I am not a stranger.
You wouldn't meet again,
But the wind, you breathe within.

I shall come back to you,
Through every rain, which falls upon
In the dark, the moon bestowed, too,
And the sun that brightens your world,
Is me under heaven.

Whom are you chasing so far,
Yet haven't abated a little mile,
Where are you trying to elude, eh?
Shadow of yours I am
Invariable.

What are you looking at?
Hear my voice through the birds,
That sing a melody dweet*,
Well, try not to forget nevertheless,
In every person you greet.
I am the one who lives!

Annotations-
dweet – divine and sweet

I Choose To Let You Go

by Vaneeta Chugh (Quing VC)

I knew someday you would leave
Still, my heart is only yours
Drifting apart is our destiny
But no matter what,
I am only yours.

I wouldn't feel ever alone,
But my love shall forever grow,
Because to you, my soul belongs,
I choose to let you go.
Baby,
I choose to let you go…

Every night my dream and companion,
The sun takes you away from me,
But after the moon shines,
You would be makin' love to me.

I wouldn't feel ever alone
But my love shall forever grow
Because to you my soul belongs
I choose to let you go,
Baby,
I choose to let you go…

I can't say I don't miss you,
Every single moment, I do,
But your happiness is what I wish,
Craving for more of you,
Oh, baby!
My love is so deep,
Still, I didn't let you drown in,
Because,
Love is never meant to hold,
You have to surrender thy soul!

I wouldn't feel ever alone,
But my love shall forever grow,
Because to you my soul belongs,
I choose to let you go,
I choose to let you go
Baby,
I choose to let you go…

A Tale Of The Forest

by Vansh Aggarwal

Dedicated to Taylor Swift and all the Swifties

Your dance with the flames
Your songs of the lore
Take me back to the day
When you held the ring
And carved my name
All along the seashore.

Every inch of your cry
Was a blue drop of gold
Alas! The time has come
For me to let you know.

Love Unvoiced

That
Weak is my will
To savour your bread
And I know that I will
Only starve to death.

But nay, your chains
Don't free me anymore
My desire and my wings
Lie yonder the seashore.

The forest is the witness
To the turn of our pages.
The forest shall recount
Our memoir to the ages.

This snow bears upon it
The footprints of our tale.
This snow shall not melt
It shall not turn to hail.

So, say what you will
But I cannot let you spill
Any more of my blood
In the shape of your heart.
Any more of my blood
In the shape of your heart.

Under Those Stars

by Samarpuneet Kaur Sandhu

What would be the one thing you'd ask for, which could be yours, forever? Mine would be you. That imperfect soul of yours would be the perfect thing for me to have in my life forever.

I look at other people's love stories and I'm reminded of my loss. I'm reminded of the love that doesn't exist in my life anymore. Would you like to help me forget about my losses? Would you like to remind me how good it feels to be loved by someone?

I know it sounds pathetic, but for once, think about it. It's us, together, walking towards a garden under the sheet of stars. You and I look at each other with nothing but love. I tell you; you look handsome, and somewhere, I get lost in your words.

Under those stars, we lie beside each other, and you hold my hand, you hold my hand so tightly and ask me to never leave your side. You wrap your arms around me and bring me close to your heart and just like that our souls become one. Doesn't it sound magical to you?

Well, guess what? I had that magical love, I had it all. But it went missing somewhere, and with it, my soul got lost, too. You know I miss the feeling so important to someone that they couldn't spend more than a few hours without you. Clingy, I know, but it felt good. I miss us sometimes. I miss you caressing my face, I miss your touch, and in all, I miss you.

Sometimes, I feel you sitting by my side with my head on your shoulder and your arm around me and I get happy for that one second. Sad, I know. I wonder sometimes if you, too, were left with some unvoiced words. I mean, till this day, I get the urge to tell you that you look better with long black messy wavy hair, or those big brown eyes is not the only beautiful feature of yours.

I believe you fall in love young, and you die young in love, but in my case, you lose your young love! It's funny how easy it is for me to write about all this but so difficult to voice it out; maybe, I'm scared that someone will hear me but then again, I want to be heard; confusing, right?

It's silly how even after almost seven hundred days, you are always on my mind. I don't know why I try to find you in other people when I know for sure I don't want 'you'. I don't understand why my heart wants you when you broke it into a million pieces and you know what, wanting you still makes my heart break even more, because I know there's no going back to how it was with us. But I guess I just have to make peace with what's left, otherwise my heart will forever be broken and my words will forever remain unheard.

I See You

by Samarpuneet Kaur Sandhu

I see you looking at me with love
I see your eyes searching for me
I see your face lighting up with just a sight of me.
And I want to say thank you!
Thank you for being you!
Thank you for making me feel as if my mere presence is enough
for you!
Thank you for looking at me with that love in your eyes!
Just so you know,
I see you too, my eyes look for you too, and my heart burns for
you, too!

Yesterday Was Beautiful

by Szuati Dube

It was not the first time I thought about telling him about my feelings. But I couldn't.

Whenever he came to my house, he greeted my parents and narrated all the tales of the war that took place on the border.

I have fallen in love ever since I saw him.

Though he was not my childhood friend as he was five years older than me, he was always there to protect me either from the 'bad' kids of our society or from the neighbour's dog.

How much I loved those days!

After he joined the force, he used to come once a year, and whenever he did, he paid us a visit.

But for the last few years, he spent most of his time at his favourite place – the border.

This reminds me how much I hate J. P. Dutta's film Border, which we watched together when we were kids.

The last time he visited us, he looked appalled.

"Aren't you enjoying it there?" I teased.

"What makes you think that?" he asked, running his fingers through his hair.

"It's visible all over your face," I said.

He sniffed. "Kavya, I can never win this. How do you come to know what I'm feeling or thinking whereas I can never guess what's on your mind?" he exclaimed.

"Maybe you are more than a family to me and for you, I am not," I mocked him.

"Idiot head! You're always family to me," he said, sliding his hand on my shoulder.

I never dared to ask him if he really meant that and wanted to add me to his family forever.

All these years when he hadn't come, I thought of all the worst-case scenarios possible, in which he loved someone else or worse, he married her, or the worst of all, which I couldn't make myself think.

But then he called his parents, and they told my parents that he would be coming home soon.

I was all happy, as now my studies were over; I could finally gather the courage to tell him about my feelings.

It was not easy, though, to tell someone how much you love them. I was scared of how our family would react but more importantly, how would he react?

If he never accepted my love, then would things be normal or the same as they were now?

I couldn't bring myself to say it to him.

But I had to, because if I didn't say it now, I would never have the chance to.

After going through thousands of self-doubts, I finally decided to not tell him then.

Maybe sometime later.

Maybe when his family was fixing him with someone else, or when he would be about to tell his family about the girl he would have been in love with for so many years.

But not now.

I decided to wait.

Finally, that day arrived.

But three years, six months, nine days later, when he finally came, all my emotions rolled out of my eyes. I couldn't make myself stand still; suddenly, my legs couldn't hold the weight of my body, my heartbeat paced faster, my mind jammed, I could not breathe even standing under the open blue sky. I sprinted through the gate. There was a heavy crowd gathered outside his house.

I couldn't see him from the middle of the crowd.

I couldn't find him.

I stepped forward, pushing everyone aside. Juggling through the crowd, I finally saw him.

There he was.

And time stopped.

His body was calmly placed in a ponderous brown wooden box wreathed in a vibrant tricolour flag.

His silent eyes were not looking for anyone, his lips were not telling any stories, and his arms were not spreading for someone.

And his face looked calm, still instead in this scorching heat.

"Major Gaurav Dalip Singh, you will always be missed."

Acknowledgements

Dear Reader,

Firstly, thank you for picking up this book. I present a token of gratitude towards all those who have played a major role in the creation of this amalgamation of articles, stories, and poems.

To begin, I am grateful to my parents for being the sole reason for my existence, my brother Chirkankshit Bihari Bulani for submitting the first piece for my anthology and standing by my side at every stage of the making of this book and my eldest brother Mr. Ishank Bulani for being the best cheerleader throughout the process.

Next, I would like to thank my two special gems – Ms. Dhruvika and Mr. Kavya Agrawal for being my biggest motivators. Also, I am really thankful to Mr. Vansh Aggarwal for being an excellent proofreader and for keeping a check on me and the progress of the anthology and Ms. Srishti Sareen, for being a great guide.

Lastly, I am extremely grateful to Inkfeathers Publishing for giving me such a great opportunity to work on this project; the Publishing Manager, Ms. Uma Bokil, and the entire Inkfeathers team for giving me such valuable support and guidance.

Thank you everyone for bringing this book to the readers.

Love,
Lokeshna Bulani

Meet the
Co-Authors

Gauri Agarwal (@ag._.gauri)

Gauri Agarwal was born on 10th May 2006. She never wrote a poem because she wanted to be a poet. She first started writing because she was confused about how she was feeling. She wanted to understand and express it beautifully, even though it was a feeling that was unfamiliar to her.

Shubhang Sharma (@shubhang.sharma.182)

Shubhang Sharma, a student of K.V. Tagore Garden, New Delhi, India, is a beginner to the poetry field. Inspired by society and parents, he took to poetry. Intense and light-hearted music motivates him to write. His caring family has always stood by him. He has also been writing Sainos. His feelings are the core of his verse, revealing deep emotions. He is the author of the book 'Art of Knitting the Life' and has served as co-author for different anthologies. Apart from poetry, his aesthetic pieces of art exhibit a genre of creativity.

Vansh Aggarwal (@end_of_the__line)

Always up for discussing art, literature, poetry, and music, maybe drift off onto a totally random and abstract topic sometimes; you'll never guess Vansh's age from his words. Hoping to stumble upon his destination someday, he's written about love, he's written about hatred, he's written about death, and he's written about life, but the hardest he's ever had to write is this bio about himself.

Sanaskriti Saha *(@nancydupain)*

Sanaskriti is a fourteen-year-old student who resides in the glorious city of joy, Kolkata. She earns herself some priority by writing whatever happens in her surroundings and in nature with some rhymes in her diary. This teen writer started writing at the age of eight through Telekids, Telegraph. Being with her own happiness and joy is the way she chooses which includes writing, reading and some music of her type. Sanaskriti's parents being her support and her diary being her best friend, she ventures a rhythmic journey of life.

Asmi Deshpande *(@asmi0809)*

Asmi Deshpande is an author and a poet who has seen the world at its worst yet persists to believe in its best. Growing up in the defence, she hasn't had a home in any one city, and this can be seen in her work's vibrant, luminescent environments. An only child, she long ago figured out how to find pleasure in her own company and being an extraordinary bookworm, it didn't take her long to begin pouring herself onto the page as an outlet for that passionate mind.

Anvi Gupta *(@_.ravenx)*

She's an interesting person, a puzzle. Once you think, "Oh, damn! How can someone write so beautifully?" She's on her quest to pen down the stories swirling in her heart. It's her boldness that defines her writing. No matter how sensitive a

subject is, she effortlessly pens her thoughts on it. All her pieces, boundless compassion, the never-ending zeal to give life to her stories, the depressive corners… there's nothing more beautiful than them.

Tiara Mehrotra *(@tiaaaa22_)*

Tiara, an eighteen-year-old was born and raised in the city of dreams, Mumbai. Tiara considers her principles and family to be the most important to her. If she isn't spending time with her loved ones, you will find her at the terrace with her guitar under the starry night, playing Taylor

Swift songs. Her future goal is to be a designer and a writer. Her life mantra is "Don't try to fit in when you were born to stand out." She is a thalassophile.

Aksheeta Chandok *(@aksheeta_chandok)*

Referred to as *"chalta phirta Bollywood"*, Aksheeta is a nineteen-year-old Delhi-ite pursuing her Bachelor's in Economics and Marketing Management, BHU, Varanasi. She finds solace in aesthetics, and you can find her clicking pictures of everything she comes across.

Vedika

Vedika, a sixteen-year-old student is a person having enthusiasm towards music, writing, art, learning new languages, travelling, photography, etc. A creative individual who loves to express herself through her words, she views life with a positive aspect. Her future goal includes being an author,

who can inspire and heal others with her words. She believes that each day is a new chance for us to chase our dreams.

Laveena Chandnani *(@usually_unusual)*

She's an eighteen-year-old who still believes in the vibe of true love. She's a nefelibata girl who lives in her own world of fantasies and imaginations. She wants her readers to know that true love still exists. Her write-ups revolve around the theme of love, where she wants to let everyone feel the vibe of love. She's a girl who respects people's flaws and she loves people who love their flaws.

Harshvi Soni

Harshvi is a person who gets in touch with her feelings through poetries. In the fast-moving city of Mumbai, she finds her inner peace and calmness in her writings. Observing, reading, and writing give her a different perspective of the world, a sense of happiness. She

is a big-time introvert and loves to explore the themes of romance, young love, and emotional attachments.

Tanisha Joshi

Tanisha Joshi, a nineteen-year-old poet/writer from Bhopal, Madhya Pradesh. She is a blend of frank mannerisms and a contemplative mind. She has always been fascinated by the human mind. She is someone who gets happy with the little things. She is a schizophrenic and likes to call herself a people's person. She likes to learn more and more with each opportunity and day. She can be contacted at joshitanisha29@gmail.com.

C. Dave

C. Dave is a fourteen-year-old girl. She is fond of reading books, dancing, and debating. Her Myers Briggs personality type is an INTJ. She believes in the quote "If you don't sacrifice for what you want, what you want becomes the sacrifice."

Sumedha Pant *(@pantsumedha)*

Sumedha, a girl from a place in the mountains, Pithoragarh, is a physiotherapist by profession and a poetess by passion. She dreams of becoming a successful therapist. Her favourite things to do are reading books and singing. She believes that words when narrated rightly can do miracles. She is a lady of words and can express every emotion perfectly.

Szuati Dube

She is a creative writer based in India. Her passion graved in reading & writing historical nonfiction stories. She can usually be found building new ideas, reading, and listening to the stories of local people.

Muskan Sahani *(@laughwithsmiley)*

Muskan is a twenty-year-old student from the city of Varanasi. She loves flowers, especially the amazing white rose. She also loves to write, read and is also very active in sports. Her dream is to be considered as an author one day. And she also wants to pursue her career in law. Her favourite line is "It's just a life, it will end before we know it."

Garv Archana *(@noob_garvv)*

The author lives in the oldest inhabited city and the land of *malaiyyo*, Varanasi. He first picked the pen up when he was nine, glad for his poor memory that he forgot to put it down. Cooking up poems and stories with his ladle of emotions is the craft with which he feeds people — a craft which has his sincerest efforts of satiating peoples' hearts.

Bhoomika Aggarwal *(@aggarwal_bhoomika1)*

"Pen down each and every moment of life as beautifully as possible, and when it comes to poetries, they are an absolutely unsurpassable way for me to represent my conception about life in a better way," believes Bhoomika. Bhoomika is currently a student and a Delhi-ite. She admires writing her feelings and perspectives about life in poetries.

Srishti Sareen *(@unconditional_sins)*

Srishti Sareen is a student of Master of Arts in English. She was born and brought up in Ludhiana. Writing is what makes her feel alive and relieved. She started writing when she was in the tenth standard, never getting over the era of satisfaction ever again. Recently, she has felt more connected to her style of poetry.

Rakhee Daryanani *(@socialswithrakhs)*

Rakhee is an aviation enthusiast and now working as a freelancer in Content Writing and Social Media Management. She is an ardent lover of travel and collecting boarding passes is her hobby. She is a devotee of Bollywood music and singing is her passion.

Vaneeta Chugh *(@yoursecretishdiary)*

Vaneeta Chugh is a graduate in B. Com and diploma in special education (visual impairment), born and brought up in Delhi. She is soaring beyond the pinnacle of her dreams. She loves penning down soulful wonders and reviving a new cosmos through her quill. Her passion is to be the legendary Wordsmith.

Tanushree Dewanjee

Tanushree, a twenty-year-old girl from a small town of Assam and hopelessly romantic as a student of English literature, became passionate about writing by reading the Brontë sisters and Austen and chose to become a writer as her future goal. For her, writing is the best way to express your love and emotions.

Ria Gandhi *(@ria._gandhi)*

Ria Gandhi is a designer, a budding entrepreneur, and an aspiring writer. To her, writing is way beyond holding a pen in her hands. She believes that authors and poets write from their souls. Writing to her is a very therapeutic process that heals not only writers but also readers.

Varsha Mahipal

This is Varsha Mahipal, from Telangana. Her writing journey started a year back, everyone has a talent they don't know about, and for her, it was writing. She never dreamt of becoming a writer, and here she is now; it just took time to express. Life has many surprises; never lose hope.

Nikunj Goyal

Nikunj Goyal is a fifteen-year-old writer. He started writing in November 2021 and was really interested in it. He has written over thirteen poems by now and over twenty quotes. To know how his work is; he started an Instagram page, @mr_talkinspire on which he posts all the content he wrote.

Bedavalli Misra *(@mrs.bedavallimisra)*

Bedavalli Misra is an alumna of Miranda House, Delhi University. She has written in a number of anthologies, on myriad themes. As a die-hard romantic, who believes in a sublime bond that entwines souls through lifetimes, she loves spinning tales of eternal and ethereal love.

Madhuchhanda Das *(@madhu2rhyme)*

Madhuchhanda, a lady from the city of joy, Kolkata, has completed her master's in library and information science and was working in a school library till 2018. As a librarian, she developed a keen interest in writing her thought journal every day after going through the pages of the books she selected for herself. She understood that reading is therapeutic and started writing everyday quotes for better understanding of life.

Love Unvoiced has given her an opportunity to pen down the most cherished and precious moments of her life (her childhood love). So, here she shares her most precious article with her target group.

Priya Debnath

Priya, a twenty-year-old girl from the state of tea garden, Assam, has taken her interest in writing by the habit of keeping her daily diary. Despite being a student of History major, she still enjoys reading English literature and hopes to pursue her career in writing.

Didriksha Chakraborty

A young poet in her teenage years who has the desire to raise her voice through her poems, she is an introvert and thus her poems serve as the best way to connect to the world. She has already participated in a few anthologies and hopes to continue doing so. She can

be contacted at chakrabortydidriksha@gmail.com.

Chirkankshit Bihari Bulani *(@art_by_cheeku)*

Chirkankshit is a peculiar teenager, and a harsh critique of orthodoxy. His prowess is his command over the English language, and his ardour for debating. His reticence is vexatious, yet he goes full on when a topic stimulates his intellect.

Apoorva Ravi *(@meandering_soul)*

Apoorva is a writer, poet, and mental health advocate. With live experience in the field of mental health, she wants to spread awareness in the field. She is also a PhD scholar, music enthusiast and loves her cats and dogs a lot.

Mansi Kothekar *(@manu_kothekar)*

Mansi is a curious, vulnerable, empathetic, courageous soul filled with love. She became a doctor by profession and has always been a writer at heart. She hopes to startle, jitter, amaze yet calm and empower you with her words.

Vaishnavi Zinjad *(@vaishnav_eeee)*

Enthusiastic, independent, artistic, outgoing, a lover of freedom and different genres of poetry, Vaishnavi loves travelling the whole world in search of ideas. Who dreams that this year all the readers will discover the joy of reading?

Namoe *(@namoephoto)*

Namoe (he/his) is a photographer-poet from the United States. He enjoys experiencing this beautiful world through images of nature and abstractions of light, and with poetry through the infinite bounds of the human soul.

Veena Antony *(@drizzlinglover)*

Veena Antony is a lawyer from Kerala whose hometown is Kochi. She is interested in writing, reading, and painting. She is very fond of spiritual books. Since school time she has been showing affection towards literature. Lots of her works are already published. Travelling and cooking are  her other passions. "Be happy and make others happy" is her motto. She likes to share her happiness among others through her works. "Celebrate and enjoy each and every moment of your life, because tomorrow is unpredictable." This is her advice to everyone.

Anu Thampy

Though professionally a nurse, she dreams to be a budding writer with exemplary thoughts and emotions expressed through writings. She believes writing is a safe and sacred way of letting out deep insights.

Nilesh Mandhyan

Nilesh is pretty much your boy next door. He usually spends his time accompanied by either books or music. He also excels in sports like basketball and athletics and loves listening to Conan Grey.

Sandhita Agarwal *(@curls.memoir)*

Sandhita is a mobile apps developer by profession but a hippie writer at heart. She likes to read and dance to goofy songs in her spare time. She lives in Bangalore with her cocker-spaniel.

Harshita Gupta *(@scribbler_musings)*

Harshita Gupta, a Psychology student and an aspiring writer, loves writing about a million unsaid feelings of her heart. She searches for solace in between her words and poetries.

Mansi Valera *(@_skyverse_)*

Mansi Valera is a twenty-year-old student of English literature born in Gujarat. She loves books, poems, and nature. She believes that kindness and good words can heal this world.

Samarpuneet Kaur Sandhu *(@samarpuneet)*

She's someone who not only sees people but hears them out, too. A movie-head would be the right way to describe her. She's not 'blah', she's a 'hoot'!

Bhumika Khandelwal *(@bhumikaaa._)*

Born in a patriarchal society, Bhumika grew up strong and unapologetic. She wishes to make "change" her first and last name because that is all she wants and represents. They say a pen is the most powerful weapon; she says, "Let's add our voice along. Let's skip qualifications in introductions and start looking for agendas."

Dev Sahu *(@aarya.dev.1217)*

Dev is a budding non-fiction writer who usually likes to write on topics that help people understand life and the world from a unique point of view.

INKFEATHERS PUBLISHING

India's Most Author Friendly Publishing House

Stay updated about the latest books, anthologies, events, exclusive offers, contests, product giveaways and other things that we do to support authors.

 Inkfeathers Publishing

 @InkfeathersPublishing

 @_Inkfeathers

 @Inkfeathers

 Inkfeathers.com

We'd love to connect with you!

www.ingramcontent.com/pod-product-compliance
Lightning Source LLC
Chambersburg PA
CBHW020340160726
47992CB00004B/1901